KARL MARX

Karl Marx

Philosophy
and Revolution

SHLOMO AVINERI

Yale

UNIVERSITY

PRESS

Yale University Press books may be purchased in quantity for educational,
business, or promotional use. For information, please e-mail sales.press@yale.edu
(U.S. office) or sales@yaleup.co.uk (U.K. office).

Set in Janson type by Integrated Publishing Solutions.
Printed in the United States of America.

ISBN 978-0-300-21170-2 (hardcover : alk. paper)
Library of Congress Control Number: 2018963640
A catalogue record for this book is available from the British Library.

This paper meets the requirements of ANSI/NISO Z39.48-1992
(Permanence of Paper).

10 9 8 7 6 5 4 3 2 1

CONTENTS

CONTENTS

Preface

BECAUSE OF HIS DARK COMPLEXION, Karl Marx was nick-named by his friends and colleagues *Der Mohr* ("The Moor"), as in *Othello*. This is how Friedrich Engels always addressed him in their voluminous correspondence—*Lieber Mohr.* This was also how Marx himself occasionally signed his own letters.

Nobody, of course, thought Marx was of Moorish or Arab descent; the playful orientalist nickname was, however, a con-stant, even if surreptitious, reminder of his family's Jewish back-ground. As far as we know, it never became a subject of public discussion, yet its presence is undeniable.

In his magisterial essay "Benjamin Disraeli, Karl Marx, and the Search for Identity," Isaiah Berlin eloquently argued that Marx's passionate advocacy for the proletariat has to be ascribed to his Jewish ancestry: "It is the oppression of centuries of a people of pariahs, not of a recently risen class, that is speaking in him." Others have claimed that it was the tradition of Old

Testament prophecy that found expression in Marx's messianic vision. Perhaps; but in the cauldron of nineteenth-century revolutionary movements, many who had no Jewish background also shared this political messianism, which could as easily have its roots in the Christian as in the Judaic tradition.

Marx cannot be seen as a "Jewish thinker," and his knowledge of matters Jewish was minimal. Nor did his biography follow any pattern of Jewish life. Yet his Jewish origins and background did leave significant fingerprints in his work, some of them obvious and others less so. One of the aims of this book is to put this background in its proper and balanced perspective.

Marx was a revolutionary thinker—philosopher, historian, sociologist, economist, current affairs journalist, and editor— not a revolutionary activist. With the exception of less than two years during the revolutions of 1848–49, he was not involved in revolutionary activities, and even that was mainly as a newspaper editor. Any biography that would try to divorce the flesh-and-blood Karl Marx from the iconic "Karl Marx" will have to focus mainly on his writings, which document his intellectual development, with all its nuances, in a much more fascinating way than the canonical image in which he is mostly presented.

This may not be an easy task. Marx's canonization and the codification of his thoughts into a doctrine called "Marxism" began quite soon after his death, led by Engels, who became the official executor of his literary legacy. Attuned to the political needs of the ascending German Social Democratic Party in the late 1880s and early 1890s, Engels was responsible for making many of Marx's works known to a wider public. This included republishing long forgotten writings, as well as deciding which of Marx's numerous manuscripts should be published. This editorial work also involved decisions about which of Marx's manuscripts would *not* be published. Consequently, many of these manuscripts were first published only half a century later, in the 1920s and 1930s; and because of the turmoil of European history at that time they did not become widely known until after World War II.

Engels also provided prefaces to Marx's writings edited and published by him, and they helped to present Marx's thoughts as a closed theoretical system, sometimes elevating occasional comments on current affairs into *ex cathedra* doctrines, as if enunciating eternal verities. Most of Marx's seminal writings have reached twentieth-century readers through these editorial efforts of Engels, and it can be easily shown that in many cases political writers, both socialists and anti-socialists, as well as scholars, attribute to Marx views and positions that originate in prefaces by Engels rather than in Marx's own texts. What is usually called "Marxism" is what Engels decided to include in the corpus and the way he interpreted it. The post-1917 schism between Social Democrats and Communists further exacerbated these intellectual gladiatorial fights over interpretation of what has sometimes become an ossified set of dogmas.

Since Marx's fame has been mostly posthumous, this biography will try to present him in the actual historical contexts, intellectual and political, in which he lived and acted. Liberating the real-life Marx from the canonization in which his thought has been wrapped helps to discover a much more exciting and compelling thinker who grew with his time and learned from the history he was living through.

When taken off his pedestal, Marx appears to grow in stature. Despite his sober assessments and setbacks, he never lost his belief in a redemptive future, anchored in the internal dialectics of historical development, regardless of how long it will take to arrive and how differing and ever-changing its form might be. And in this belief he was proven both right and wrong.

KARL MARX

1

Jew? Of Jewish Origin? A Converted Jew?

LESS THAN TWO MONTHS after Karl Marx's death in London in March 1883, his youngest daughter, Eleanor ("Tussy") Marx-Aveling, published in the socialist journal *Progress* an obituary of her father. In the second paragraph she wrote: "Karl Marx was born at Trier on May 5, 1818, of Jewish parents. His father—a man of great talent—was a lawyer, strongly imbued with the French eighteenth-century ideas of religion, society, and the arts; his mother was the descendant of Hungarian Jews who in the seventeenth century settled in Holland."

Marx's Jewish background was of course common knowledge, but he never referred to it publicly himself, certainly not in the way described here. Yet explicitly bringing up her father's Jewish origin in such a prominent way should not come as a surprise from Eleanor. Of Marx's three daughters, she was the best educated and the most active politically. She was also an essayist and a prolific translator of both literary and political works: she translated Flaubert's *Madame Bovary* into English, as well as Ibsen's plays *The Enemy of the People, The Wild Duck,* and *The Pillars of Society,* George Plekhanov's *Anarchy and Socialism,* and Eduard Bernstein's biography of Ferdinand Lassalle. Among her own writings was a study of the working-class movement in America and a feminist tract, *The Woman Question.* As part of her activities among working-class people in London's East End, many of them recent Jewish immigrants from eastern Europe, she learned Yiddish. On one memorable occasion she declared, in Yiddish, "I am one of you," and on another she accepted an invitation to address a rally protesting Russian anti-Jewish policies and pogroms, adding "I shall be more glad as my father was a Jew."

Yet for all this, and despite writing with warmth and pride about her father's Jewishness, her description in the obituary overlooks most of the defining moments of her family history.

Even as Eleanor stated that both of her father's parents were Jewish and praised Karl Marx's father for being imbued with French Enlightenment ideas about religion, she refrained from mentioning that he had converted to Christianity, and she also did not address the circumstances of his conversion. By prominently referring to her father's Jewish background, she made an important point, but she totally missed—or perhaps intentionally avoided—the personal drama, historical significance, and possible traumatic memories of the odyssey that turned Karl Marx, the grandson of two rabbis, into one of the most influential revolutionary thinkers of the nineteenth century. And therein lies a story, the historical significance of which transcends Marx's personal biography.

PARADISE LOST

Karl Heinrich Marx was born on 5th May 1818, in Trier in the Rhineland, then part of the kingdom of Prussia. Founded by the Romans as Augusta Treverorum and considered the oldest town in Germany, Trier is deeply steeped in history, displaying some famous Roman monuments, among them the exquisite Porta Nigra, the largest Roman edifice north of the Alps.

For almost two thousand years the Rhineland has also been the center of the Jewish presence in the German lands. In the wake of the Roman legions, Jewish merchants crossed the Alps and established themselves along the Rhine, the main regional artery of commerce and communications. In documents written mostly in Hebrew, these thriving Jewish communities retained the echoes of the Latin names of their cities—*Magenza* (Mogontiacum/Mainz), *Shpeira* (Spira/Speyer), *Vermaiza* (Augusta Vangionum/Worms). In the twelfth century, an assembly of rabbis and scholars from the Rhineland set down a compendium of internal decrees regulating the structures, institutional arrangements, and functions of Jewish communities. This set of regulations, known as Takanot SHUM (the Hebrew acronym for the names of the three leading Rhenish communities) was over time adopted by many other communities and became the template for the way Jewish self-governing institutions fitted into the feudal and corporate life of medieval Europe.

In 1096, the First Crusade brutally interrupted Jewish life in the Rhineland. While the gentry-led crusaders, headed by Geoffrey of Bouillon, set out for the Holy Land from northern France and Flanders, hordes of what became known as the People's Crusade assembled in the region of the lower Rhine, and set on their road to the East, marching up the river. Egged on by populist preachers, like the legendary Peter the Hermit, they visited violence and destruction on the Jewish communities along their route, including on the Jews of Trier. The papal call to liberate the holy sites of Christendom in Jerusalem from Muslim rule was transformed into horrendous massacres of the Jewish population of the Rhineland—the first massive anti-Jewish riots in western Europe. The official church hierarchy was so shocked by this anti-Jewish violence that some bishops and archbishops opened their compounds to protect the local Jewish community from the wrath of the fanatical Christian rabble, and in some cases themselves became victims of the religious demon unleashed by the call to protect Christianity's holy sites in the Orient.

These traumas remained deeply etched in the collective Jewish memory over generations: some of the laments written under the impact of these harrowing events are still being recited on the High Holidays; and the year 1096 (4856 according to the Hebrew calendar) is seen as a watershed in European Jewish history, heralding later anti-Jewish legislation and persecution.

But the Jewish communities in the Rhineland largely survived and continued to flourish. The rise of the Christian burgher class in the late Middle Ages brought about municipal anti-Jewish legislation, when many so-called Free Cities in the Holy Roman Empire adopted the Magdeburg Statutes, which included the *Privilegium de non tolerandis Iudaeis*, or right to exclude Jews. This caused many cities in the German lands to expel Jews, although in the Rhineland these expulsions were mostly temporary, and the historical communities continued their existence. Many Jews, however, moved farther east, to the more tolerant Polish-Lithuanian commonwealth, which eventually became the largest region of Jewish presence in Europe.

It was the French Revolution and its consequences that dramatically changed the fortunes of the Jews in the Rhineland. On the eve of the revolution, the Rhineland was a patchwork of petty jurisdictions: principalities and duchies, markgraviates and landgraviates, counts palatine and imperial free cities, archiepiscopal sees exercising secular jurisdiction, independent knights and minor baronies—the region was a kaleidoscope, signifying the ultimate decrepitude of the medieval idea of a universal empire.

The French Revolution and later the Napoleonic wars brought major changes to the region. French armies occupied the Rhineland, did away with the multitude of local jurisdictions, annexed most of the region to France, and later, under Napoleon, set up the kingdom of Westphalia farther east, with Napoleon's brother Jérome on its throne.

Like most of the Rhineland, Trier was thus annexed to the French Republic and later became part of the Napoleonic empire, with political, social, and intellectual consequences that are still visible in the area today. One of the immediate and far-reaching results had to do with the status of the Jews.

Revolutionary France was the first European country to emancipate its Jews, granting them equal political and civic rights. When it annexed the Rhineland, this emancipation was extended to Jews there as well, and the Jewish population was transformed from a tolerated but not equal community into full and equal citizenship. Limits on Jewish professional activity and landowning were lifted, as were restrictions on residence rights; schools and universities were opened to Jewish students, as was the civil service. For the first time Jews could serve as lawyers, judges, doctors, military officers, and civil servants. As evidenced in Jewish prayers, sermons, and poems of the time, many Jews saw this as an almost messianic redemption, and republican France—and later Napoleon—were praised as a modern, secular incarnation of the messianic vision. The twenty years between the mid-1790s and 1814 witnessed the appearance for the first time—in France as well as in the annexed Rhineland—of Jewish persons as equal citizens, active in the professions and in general social and political life. France, in its extended borders, was viewed as the new, modern Promised Land, a secular paradise in the here and now, established on the hallowed grounds of Enlightenment and Emancipation.

This came to a cruel end in 1814–15 following the defeat of Napoleon, and the Congress of Vienna, which set up the borders and contours of post-revolutionary and post-Napoleonic Europe: the Restoration, identified with the politics of the leading Austrian statesman Prince Metternich. France was set back more or less to its pre-1789 borders and lost the territories it had annexed, including the Rhineland.

It was obvious that the patchwork of pre-revolutionary political systems in the Rhineland could not be revived. Instead, most of this territory was annexed to Prussia, as a reward for its role in the anti-Napoleonic coalition. This changed Prussia in many respects: from a marginal, middle-sized eastern kingdom it became a much bigger country controlling large expanses of territory bordering on France; from a mainly agricultural land, dominated by its Junker class, it gained regions with a traditional commercial culture, also rich in the mineral resources of the Ruhr; and from a predominantly Protestant country, with a Lutheran state church, it gained a large Catholic population. Last, and not least, significant numbers of Jews, in the historical Rhenish communities, were added to it, outnumbering the small Jewish population in the traditional Prussian and Brandenburg lands of the east.

But the Jewish population of the new Rhenish territories differed fundamentally from the Jews then residing in the original Prussian provinces, and this presented the Prussian authorities with some tricky problems in their new domains. In Prussia proper, the Jewish religion was tolerated and Jews were protected, but they were not equal under the law. Despite some liberal legislation introduced by the Prussian reforms associated with Baron Karl vom Stein and Karl August von Hardenberg in the early 1800s, there were still restrictions on where Jews could live as well as limitations on land ownership, and they were not allowed to join the free professions. Prussia was faced with a novel dilemma, as with the territory came people: emancipated Jews in the Rhineland, who enjoyed equal rights with their Christian neighbors, served as lawyers, judges, and civil servants. People still remembered how the first well-known Jewish philosopher, Moses Mendelssohn, needed a special royal dispensation to reside in Berlin in the late 1700s. True, there were some moneyed, privileged Court Jews and financiers in Prussia, like the Ephraim family, who owned palatial residences —but Jews as such did not enjoy equal rights in what was considered a Christian state.

Anticipating the possible consequences of the annexation of the Rhineland to Prussia, a Jewish delegation, headed by the leaders of the Jewish community in Frankfurt (then as now a center of banking), went to Vienna and petitioned Metternich not to revoke the rights of Jews who had enjoyed twenty years of civic equality under French rule, but to no avail. The matter was referred to the decision of the new authorities now established under the arrangements of the Congress of Vienna.

After some deliberations, the Prussian authorities in the Rhineland revoked Jewish emancipation and imposed on the Jews in the newly annexed territories the status of Jews in Prussia proper. The major principle, following the precepts of what it meant to be a Christian state, implied that Jews could not be in a situation of authority over Christians: they could not serve as lawyers, judges, civil servants, teachers in schools or universities. In other words, the Rhenish Jews were de-emancipated, thrown back to where they—or their parents—had been a generation ago.

Among the tremendous consequences of the post-1815 Restoration, the change in the status of Rhenish Jews was obviously a minor and marginal footnote, and is hardly noted or mentioned by historians, but it gave rise to a totally new situation, affecting a few thousand Jews who within one generation were both granted emancipation and then drastically denied it, something that had never happened until that time to any Jewish group. The fact that most of those affected were, almost by definition, educated professional middle-class people, for whom emancipation had opened the road to being full-fledged citizens in an open society and were now thrown back into almost a medieval status, had far-reaching consequences.

In the years between 1815 and 1848 one can discern a deep feeling of alienation and consequent political radicalization among members of the Jewish intelligentsia in the Rhineland and the emergence among them—much more than among the more quietistic Jewish communities in Prussia proper—of radical politics; some did convert under that pressure, but this did not make them more supportive of the system imposed on them; others, while distancing themselves from orthodox Judaism, did try to maintain their Jewish identity in one way or another. But it is among them that one finds the pioneers of radical democracy, revolutionary socialism, and a profound critique of bourgeois society and German nationalism. Many of them exiled themselves to Paris—which not only symbolized the legacy of the Enlightenment and the French Revolution in general, but must have also meant to them the homeland that once granted to their families and ancestors equality and citizenship. No region of Germany produced so many revolutionary radicals as the Rhineland.

Among these was the revolutionary thinker and poet Heinrich Heine (born in Düsseldorf in 1799); the communist and later forerunner of Zionism Moses Hess (born in Bonn in 1812); the writer and satirist Ludwig Börne (born in Frankfurt in 1786; his father, the banker Jakob Baruch, had headed the Jewish delegation that pleaded futilely with the Congress of Vienna not to revoke the emancipation of the Rhineland Jews).

And of course, Karl Marx, son of the Trier lawyer Heinrich (Heschel) Marx.

THE FATHER: TRIBULATIONS OF A JEWISH ADVOCATE

Mordechai Levi, Karl Marx's paternal grandfather, was born in 1746 in Postolopty/Postelberg in Bohemia, and after being ordained as a rabbi moved to Trier, where he served as chief rabbi until his death in 1804. It was during his years in office that Trier was annexed to France and its Jewish population emancipated and granted equal civic rights.

This process was slowly also being reflected in the adoption of non-Jewish names, as well as what was known as "civil" surnames as required by French law. Thus we find Rabbi Mordechai Levi being referred to in official French documents first as "Marcus Levi" and then as "Marx Levi"; to this appellation his father's name (Shmuel/Samuel) was occasionally added as a patronymic, so he is sometimes referred to as "Samuel Marx Levi." In the December 1801 census under French administration he appears as "Marx Lewy, rabin" and in another document from 1803 as "Marx Levy, Rabin de la religion hébraique." Yet on his gravestone in the Jewish cemetery of Trier his Hebrew epitaph reads "Rabbi Mordechai Halevi, son of Rabbi Shmuel from Pastelburg."

This fluidity of names becomes even more evident when it comes to his son, Karl Marx's father. He is first mentioned in an extant document in the 1801 census as "Heschel Lewy," son of rabbi Marx Lewy. But with the progress of emancipation, his name changes subtly but significantly when he starts to study law. A matriculation document from the Imperial University of Coblenz in 1813 refers to him as "Henry Marx, fils de Marcus Samuel Levy," thus definitely establishing "Marx" as his surname. It may be beside the point, but it is still intriguing to speculate that had it not been for the French insistence that Jews embrace "civil" surnames rather than variations on their patronymics, Karl Marx would have been born Karl Levi. Would a theory called "Levism," or later "Levism-Leninism" have the same appeal and resonance as "Marxism"? The haunting question "what's in a name" may echo here as well.

There is a further, though minor, shift in the father's name with the advent of the Prussian annexation of the Rhineland: in

November 1814 the new authorities issued a passport to the young lawyer, with the German version of his name—"Heinrich Marx." He needed the passport to travel to Nijmegen in the Netherlands, where on 22nd November 1814 he married Henriette Presborg, the daughter of the local rabbi Isaac Presborg and a distant cousin on his mother's side. The marriage certificate, issued under French civil law and written in French, following two decades of French rule, referred to the bridegroom with the Dutch version of his name, Hendrick. It would not come as a surprise that with both bride and bridegroom being children of rabbis, a Jewish wedding ceremony took place a week later. All of this occurred against the background of the tremendous political upheavals following the collapse of the Napoleonic empire and the drawing of new borders by the Congress of Vienna.

It was the annexation of Trier to Prussia that confronted the young advocate with an unexpected dilemma. The new Prussian authorities decreed that Jewish civil servants and lawyers in the annexed Rhenish provinces could keep their positions— if they converted to Christianity. This would put their status on par with the situation in Prussia proper. To the Prussian authorities this must have seemed a reasonable and decent provision— no one was arbitrarily deprived of his livelihood, after all, and individuals were given a choice. To Heinrich, of course, it looked much different: he was the son of the previous local rabbi, and his brother was now the chief rabbi of Trier; he was also married to a rabbi's daughter and had many relatives in town and in the region.

Heinrich repeatedly petitioned the Prussian authorities to allow him to maintain his position as a lawyer, which he had practiced for years, arguing that although he was born to a Jewish family, he was not then a member of the Jewish community; to assure the authorities that he was nonetheless not a dangerous revolutionary atheist, he declared himself a deist and a believer in Divine Providence. Advocate Heinrich Marx published a number of learned articles in legal journals and presented them to the Prussian ministry to prove his qualifications. A friendly Prussian district commissioner even recommended to Berlin to allow Heinrich Marx—"a loyal subject"—to be exempted, together with two other Jewish lawyers, from the general edict making it mandatory for advocates to be members of a Christian denomination.

This correspondence, some of it preserved in local and central Prussian archives, went back and forth for several years, as the Prussian administration slowly brought the Rhine provinces under the general, orderly Prussian system. But it was to no avail: after having exhausted all options, and needing to care for a growing family, Heinrich capitulated and decided to convert.

But the conversion was carried out in an unusual fashion, as it was obviously done most reluctantly and under protest. Trier, like most of the Rhineland, was mainly Catholic, but Heinrich decided to convert not to Roman Catholicism, but to Lutheran Protestantism. Since there was no Protestant church in Trier at the time, however, he sought out the Lutheran military chaplain and "Divisional Preacher" of the Prussian garrison just outside Trier, the Reverend Johann Heinrich Mühlenhof. Not exactly a typical act of assimilation or wish to join the majority population.

There is some uncertainty about the exact date of the conversion. Because it took place not in a regular parish church but in a military encampment, no document survived, although the name of the military chaplain who officiated has been preserved. The possible dates range from 1816 to 1819: in the first case, Karl, born in 1818, came into the world when his father was already a convert (albeit clearly a reluctant one); in the latter, and from internal evidence the more plausible date, both of Karl's parents were still at least nominally Jewish when he was born.

Heinrich's wife, Henriette, Karl's mother, did not convert

with her husband, since there was no external reason for her to do so, and apparently no need to cause unnecessary pain to her father. Only in 1825, after her father, the rabbi in the Netherlands, died, did Henriette convert. In her baptism certificate she is described as an "Israelitin," presented to the pastor by "her husband, Advocate Heinrich Marx, who had already converted." It was on this occasion that their children, including Karl, were also baptized.

Regardless of Heinrich's exact date of conversion, there is no doubt that Henriette was not yet converted to Christianity when Karl was born, so according to the strict matrilineal principles of the Halacha, or Jewish law, Karl Marx was unquestionably born Jewish.

To this unusual family story a footnote should be added, providing further evidence of how complicated and paradoxical things could be. Heinrich's brother, Samuel Marx, was ordained a rabbi and inherited his father's role as chief rabbi of Trier, a position he held until his own death in 1827. The Jewish community of Trier needed a lawyer, and since Jews could not serve as advocates, it had to choose a Christian one. Rabbi Samuel Marx chose his (Christian) brother Heinrich Marx, who for decades represented the Trier Jewish community regularly before the authorities and in numerous court cases. The two brothers, who also lived close by each other, obviously remained in constant contact.

The most extraordinary thing about this family odyssey—a chapter in the challenges of modernization facing Jewish communities and individual Jews in the wake of the French Revolution and the Restoration—is that there is no clue of it in the enormous body of work, drafts, and correspondence of Karl Marx; there is no way of reconstructing how this history was lived, and remembered, in the Marx family. Recovering its details is possible only by sifting through archives in Trier and other state and church records.

The Jewish origins of Heinrich Marx's family were of course known in a small town like Trier, but how much did Karl Marx know about his uncle, the officiating chief rabbi of Trier, or about both of his rabbinical grandfathers? Obviously some aspects of family history had to be shared. Did the two brothers, the rabbi and the Christian advocate of the Jewish community, who for years had close professional contacts, also meet socially—something almost unavoidable given their close proximity? We do not know, nor do we know how much Marx knew about the circumstances of his family's conversion. But obviously he must have known something. One can only speculate about the silence, which may or may not speak for itself: if the circumstances of the conversion were a wound, it remained at least ostensibly unknown to outsiders.

BEGINNINGS: FROM LAW STUDENT TO PHILOSOPHICAL RADICAL

Karl Marx's childhood and early youth seem uneventful and appear to have followed the pattern of what could be expected of the son of a relatively comfortable middle-class family. The spacious family home—now the site of the Karl-Marx Haus in central Trier—shows the solid social standing of his father's position as a lawyer. At the age of twelve Karl entered the local classical Friedrich Wilhelm Gymnasium, named after the reigning Prussian monarch. After graduating, he enrolled in the law faculty of the neighboring University of Bonn in October 1836, but after one year, the following October, he transferred to the law faculty at Berlin University.

This involved not only a move from provincial Bonn to the Prussian capital: it also opened the young student to what was then the most exciting and forward-looking intellectual and political ambience in Germany. Berlin University, founded in 1809 as part of the far-reaching reforms the Prussian state undertook after its crushing defeat at the hands of Napoleon's army in the Battle of Jena in 1806, was the first modern university established in Germany. It was also the first university in Europe—except the modern institutions of higher learning founded in France after the revolution—that was free from the ecclesiastical legacy of all the older European universities.

Under the guidance of the philosopher and linguist Wilhelm von Humboldt, modern teaching methods, especially in the natural sciences, were introduced; independent research was encouraged; in the humanities, such luminaries as Johann Gottlieb Fichte, Friedrich Schleiermacher, Friedrich Karl von Savigny, and G. W. F. Hegel—who all had problems fitting into the antiquated system of the traditional universities—were offered prestigious chairs. This drew to the new university some of the brightest students from all over the German lands.

The innovative atmosphere of a university situated in a modern metropolis, and not in sleepy though charming medieval towns like Göttingen, Heidelberg, Tübingen, or—for that matter—Bonn, encouraged among students, exposed to modern ideas of philosophy or law, a fervent intellectual climate leading to nonconformity and political activity. The philosophy and law taught at the university were basically conservative—but modernizing, in the spirit of the defensive reform policies introduced into the Prussian state system by leaders like vom Stein and Hardenberg: peasant vassalage was abolished, as were medieval craft guilds and corporations; cities received modern charters, education was mostly freed from church supervision, and many of the residential restrictions on the Jewish population were lifted. The modern classical gymnasium and the modern research university had their origins in these Prussian reforms, which tried to counter the waves raised by the French Revolution by substituting for the medieval feudal order a modernizing bureaucracy whose conservative aims were coupled with a careful rationalist liberalizing practice.

The young Karl Marx had already been exposed to these

currents in Trier, through his father's friendship with the top Prussian official in the city, Ludwig von Westphalen. Coming from a gentry family with traditions of public service in various German principalities, von Westphalen had initially served in the French-dominated modernizing administrations of the Rhineland during the Napoleonic period. After 1815, he was accepted into the Prussian civil service and appointed to Trier, where the mainly Catholic population, exposed to French Enlightenment ideas during French rule, presented the Prussian, Protestant administration—including von Westphalen—with a delicate task. It would not be surprising that he found a kindred soul in his neighbor, the lawyer Heinrich Marx, from a Jewish background and a graduate of French legal training; eventually the relationship spread also to the younger members of both families.

In von Westphalen, the young Marx found not only a spiritual mentor, but also his future fiancée and wife, Jenny von Westphalen, four years his senior. The two developed a deep relationship that took a few years—and a heated correspondence—to blossom into marriage. For Marx, the Westphalen connection was also a window into a wider world, and even Jenny's anglicized name suggested broader horizons: her mother, Jean Wishart, was of Scottish origin and a distant relation of the duke of Argyll. In an ironic future twist, which none of the persons involved were aware of at the time, Jenny's brother (and Karl Marx's future brother-in-law) Ferdinand von Westphalen was to become a Prussian conservative civil servant and served as Prussia's minister of interior during 1850–58, when Marx was a revolutionary exile in London. On the other hand, Jenny's other brother, Edgar, would move in revolutionary circles and was to become close to the League of Communists.

Marx's enrollment in the law faculty was a clear indication that he was initially destined to follow in his father's steps. Yet in Berlin he got involved with a group of students and young lecturers who, under the influence of Hegel's philosophy, developed a critical approach to politics, society, and religion. They were known as the Doktoren-Klub, which became the breeding ground for what eventually developed into the group of radical "Young Hegelians": among them were Bruno and Edgar Bauer, Arnold Ruge, and others who later became Marx's colleagues—and eventual adversaries.

From the correspondence between Karl Marx in Berlin and his father back in Trier it becomes clear that the father has discerned the growing interests of his son in critical philosophy and radical ideas; he occasionally voiced concerns that Karl might be sidetracked from his future career as a lawyer. The father expressed his concerns in a muted and tactful way, and for some time the son avoided responding to these strictures. Eventually he gently told his father that he was troubled by the gap between the "ought" and the "is," which German philosophy inherited from Kant. Being exposed to Hegel's philosophy, he found the answers in actual reality itself, "since the Gods which have until now dwelt above the earth . . . have now moved to its center." And in an aphorism he wrote down in a scrapbook he kept at the time he similarly declared, a bit grandly, "Kant and Fichte reach for eternal heights/ Look there for a distant land/ But I just try to comprehend/ That which I found on the street." The turning away from German idealist philosophy, with its avoidance of dealing with historical reality, is already clearly discernible.

Heinrich Marx died in October 1837. Marx's record of studies for the following semester shows that he was already abandoning his legal studies and switching to more and more courses in philosophy.

Despite his participation in the Doktoren-Klub, Marx was not involved in any clandestine activities. His record of studies, issued on 8th March 1841 by the rector and the Senate of Berlin University, also attests that "Mr Carl Heinrich Marx, born in Trier, son of the late Advocate Marx . . . has not been accused of taking part in forbidden associations among students in this university." In good Prussian bureaucratic fashion, this academic record of studies is countersigned by Messrs. Lichtenstein and Krause, "the acting representatives of the Royal Government"— that is, police officials.

2

Transcending Hegel

THE PERSON WHO INTRODUCED Marx to Hegel's philosophy was Eduard Gans, one of his teachers at Berlin University. Gans's own life reflects the tensions between the promises of modernity and the constraints of political reality and their impact on young emancipated Jews in post-1815 Germany.

Born to a Jewish banking family in Berlin, Gans studied philosophy and law, first in Berlin and then with Hegel in Heidelberg. When Hegel moved to Berlin University in 1818, Gans followed him and became his assistant and close collaborator. At the same time, together with Leopold Zunz and Heinrich Heine, Gans founded the Verein für Kultur und Wissenschaft der Juden (Society for the Culture and Study of the Jews). Established in the wake of the Hep-Hep riots—the first anti-Jewish riots in modern German history, in 1819—the society's aim was twofold: to promote a critical study of the history and culture of the Jews as a national entity, linked to a religious tradition but not subsumed under it, while at the same time enabling Jews to integrate into modern German society. The intrinsic tensions between these two aims were evident and led eventually after a few years to the demise of the society, but its pioneering attempt to present Judaism not as a mere religion but as a historical national entity had an enormous impact on Jewish intellectual discourse, and marked the beginnings of the modern, scholarly study of Jewish history and religion.

Under Hegel's tutelage, Gans's academic career progressed step by step, but was hampered by his Jewishness; temporary appointments were possible, but not a tenured position as *Ordinarius* (full professor). Gans's father, Abraham, who was the financial adviser of the reforming Prussian minister von Hardenberg, persuaded the minister to try to issue an edict exempting "unusually gifted personages" from the regulations that required university professors—as civil servants under Prussian law—to belong to a Christian denomination. But these attempts failed, and after much soul-searching—and an extended stay in Paris, where he was feted by French liberal intellectuals—Gans converted to the Lutheran Church in 1825. A year later he was appointed professor of legal philosophy at Berlin University.

Gans's conversion became a cause célèbre in Berlin intellectual circles, and even prompted Heinrich Heine, his erstwhile colleague at the Verein, to pen one of his most acerbic short poems, "To an Apostate": "And you crawled towards the cross/That same cross which you detested . . . / Yesterday you were a hero/But today you're just a scoundrel." Heine himself converted later the same year, and the anger (and disgust) may have been aimed at himself as well.

There is a wider context to Hegel's support for Gans's career. As early as 1818 Hegel called in his *Philosophy of Right* for full and equal civic and political rights for Jews, and made the point repeatedly in his university lectures. In the modern state,

Hegel argued, "it is part of education [*Bildung*] that . . . man counts as a man in virtue of his humanity alone, and not because he is a Jew, Catholic, Protestant, German, Italian, etc." At a time when all German student fraternities (*Burschenschaften*) excluded Jews as "foreigners," one of Hegel's assistants at Heidelberg, Friedrich Wilhelm Carové, was instrumental, under his teacher's influence and quoting his writings, in convincing the members of the Heidelberg fraternity to accept Jews—the only fraternity to do so at the time. It is no wonder that when Hegel moved to Berlin, he drew to his lectures many of the Jewish students there, as his advocacy for Jewish emancipation was an exception among the faculty. Gans's presence was just an outward symbol of Hegel's position, which—together with his positive evaluation of Benedict Spinoza's philosophy—drew criticism, some of it crude, of his "Judaizing" tendencies: his seminar was occasionally referred to as a "Jewish den," with "Gans, Arrogance and Absalom" dominating it.

When Hegel died in 1831, Gans was appointed to his chair and was instrumental in establishing his philosophical legacy, especially in developing the liberal—albeit conservative—elements of Hegel's political thought. He initiated the first edition of Hegel's *Werke*, and his edition of the *Rechtsphilosophie* includes as "Additions" [*Zusätze*] also the oral comments Hegel added in his lectures to the written text of his book. These "Additions" are especially significant in the sections dealing with political institutions, and were much more liberal than the published text of the book, which appeared after all under the restrictive censorship of the reactionary Carlsbad Decrees, adopted by the German states after the nationalist student outbursts that culminated in the assassination of the poet August von Kotzebue by a nationalist student and the book-burning associated with the Wartburg Festival commemorating the tercentenary of Luther's Reformation.

Gans viewed the post-1815 reformed Prussian state as a

model of a modern constitutional monarchy, and in his classes used Hegel as a yardstick by which to judge contemporary states and their road to modernity. He was also the first person in Germany to write about the Saint-Simonians, and thus helped acquaint his readers and students—Marx included—with the beginning of French socialism. His classes contributed to the ferment that eventually crystallized as the Young Hegelian school; it also led the followers of this school to the study of the criticism of religion offered by Ludwig Feuerbach and David Friedrich Strauss.

Marx attended Gans's classes for several semesters, and he mentions Gans and his lectures frequently in his notes and letters from this period. Whether he ever was able to approach his teacher on a personal level and perhaps discuss the circumstances of his conversion—so similar to those of his own father—is not known and probably would have been difficult, given the traditional German professorial distance between teachers and students. But the background story of Gans's career was common knowledge and could not have escaped Marx's attention.

Gans died in 1839, at the early age of forty-one, and Marx's official record of studies at the university shows that he virtually dropped out of the university for a couple of semesters following his professor's death. He resumed attending classes only a year later, and during this caesura his mother—by this time widowed—anxiously enquired whether he was about to finish his studies and present his much planned doctoral dissertation.

At that time Marx's reading notes suggest an increasing interest in modern philosophy—he read the works of Spinoza, Gottfried Wilhelm Leibniz, and David Hume—but for his doctoral dissertation he chose a rather esoteric subject from classical Greek philosophy: the difference between the Epicurean and Democritean philosophies of nature. Yet he did not present his dissertation to Berlin University. The absence of Gans was obviously a major reason for this, as the faculty of philosophy at Berlin was becoming much more conservative and theologically oriented, with the Hegelian element almost totally disappearing after the death of Gans.

Instead, Marx sent his dissertation to the University of Jena, which allowed external candidates to qualify for a doctorate. In April 1841 his thesis was approved by the dean of the faculty of philosophy at Jena, and he received his doctorate.

Marx's doctoral dissertation bears an extraordinarily warm dedication to his mentor and future father-in-law, Ludwig von Westphalen. Marx refers to him as his "dear fatherly friend," goes on to praise him as "a living proof that idealism is no illusion but a truth," and presents the thesis to him as "a small proof of my love and admiration to an older man who possesses the strength of youth." This may all sound like conventional flattery, but given what we know about the relationship between the two, it seems to express a deeper and genuine gratitude. There is little doubt that Marx found in Westphalen the kind of spiritual and intellectual stimulus that his own father, for all of his legal training, appeared to have lacked.

THE *RHEINISCHE ZEITUNG* AND THE BEGINNINGS OF SOCIAL CRITIQUE

Following the acceptance of his dissertation, it was time for Marx to choose his future career. The option of a civil service position, which his university education qualified him for, was something he never seriously considered. He returned to Trier and then followed Bruno Bauer—who lost his temporary position in Berlin after Gans's death—to Bonn, possibly considering a teaching position himself. Yet political developments in the Rhineland steered him in another direction. Through the circle around Bruno Bauer he met Moses Hess, who was involved in plans to set up a newspaper, *Die Rheinische Zeitung*, supported by liberal Rhenish industrialists and gathering around it a group of writers and intellectuals, many of them former students of Hegel and his disciples. In April 1842 Marx started contributing articles to the paper, and in October he was appointed its editor. He remained in the post until March 1843, when the paper was closed down by the Prussian authorities.

The *Rheinische Zeitung* was not an outspoken opposition paper, nor did it intend to be one. It viewed itself as identified with the Prussian reforms of Stein and Hardenberg, but with the accession to the throne in 1840 of Friedrich Wilhelm IV, Prussian politics changed in a much more conservative, Christian, and medievalist Romantic direction. Marx's articles in the paper —his first published writings—no doubt contributed to the authorities' view of the paper as too critical if not subversive.

On the surface, Marx's articles did not attack government policies head on. Instead, what he did in most of them was to confront recent legislation and politics with the principles of a constitutional *Rechtsstaat*, or rule of law, sometimes using Hegelian philosophical arguments.

Although Marx's articles are occasionally couched in dense philosophical terminology and arguments, they do relate to current affairs. A series of articles follows debates about property rights in the Rhenish provincial Diet. Marx argues that the Diet, elected on the basis of limited suffrage, should according to its constitutional logic represent the ideas of the general interests of society, as expressed in Hegel's theory of the state. Instead, he argues, looking at the debates and legislative decisions of the Diet, it becomes clear that it is not the general interests of society that are being promulgated, but the particularistic interests of the wealthier and stronger classes. In other words, the claim of the state to represent general interests is false: it is nothing else than the instrument of the dominant classes in civil society. Significantly, he signs some of the articles in this series by the pseudonym "Ein Rheinländer."

Another series of articles criticized the Historical School of

Jurisprudence, identified with von Savigny, the conservative law professor at Berlin whose major tenet was denying the legitimacy of universal norms of jurisprudence and arguing for the dominance of historically transmitted legal traditions, whose very longevity and ancient origin grant them their power. Hegel's *Philosophy of Right* was written partially as a polemic against this historicist, Burkean position.

Another article criticized recent Prussian censorship regulations, which brought about the closure of some newspapers (and eventually were used to ban the *Rheinische Zeitung* itself). Here the argument also follows Hegel's justification of a free press as the expression of the variety of interests and points of views that is crucial for the eventual emergence of policies aimed at the common good. Another series of articles deals with the recent retrograde Prussian divorce laws, which Marx criticized for putting property rights above individual personal rights. He also published an article on the poverty of the peasants in the Moselle Valley, where Trier is situated.

Although the articles were mild in tone, despite Marx's criticism of government policies, the one theme running through them is a censure of the state as not really representing the general interests—a theme he was to come back to in the more theoretical essays published some time later.

A few months after the closure of the *RZ*, despite his lack of gainful employment, Marx married his fiancée, Jenny von Westphalen. This was the conclusion of a lengthy and intensive courtship, which was accompanied by numerous passionate letters, poems, and dedications. This was all in the spirit of the then prevailing romantic notions of love and affection, yet the steadfastness of their relationship did survive the hardships that later befell the family in its peregrinations caused by Marx's political activities and attests to the depth of the feelings underlying the relationship despite everything.

Later family reminiscences reveal that some members of

the Westphalen family were not enthusiastic about the match: the age difference, Marx's unclear career prospects, the burden of his political associations with the Young Hegelians and the banned *RZ*, probably also his Jewish origins. But Jenny's father, true to his liberal principles and years'-long fatherly approach to Marx (especially after Heinrich Marx's death), prevailed. Ludwig von Westphalen himself died in March 1842, having approved the match and accepted Marx as his future son-in-law, and the young couple married in the neighboring resort town of Kreuznach on 19th June 1843. They spent several weeks at the resort, where Jenny's mother had been living since her husband's death. A few months later, not before some rather tense and ugly disagreements between Marx and his mother about his part in his father's inheritance, documented both in Marx's letters to his colleagues as well as in court papers, the couple left for Paris. Other than a short interval during the 1848–49 revolution, they never returned permanently to live in Germany.

It was during the summer months of 1843 spent at Bad Kreuznach—in fact an extended honeymoon—that Marx launched his first intensive critique of Hegel's political philosophy. Writing in March of that year to his colleague Arnold Ruge, Marx mentioned his intention to follow Feuerbach's critique of Hegel, but commenting that while Feuerbach focused too much on nature, the point is to move on to the critique of politics, as "it is politics which happens to be the only link through which contemporary philosophy can become actual."

This is what Marx sets out to do in thirty-nine sheets of his critique of Hegel's *Philosophy of Right* (paragraphs 261–313) that are the core of his political philosophy. These comments, later known as the *Kreuznach Notebooks* and published for the first time only in 1927, provide a rare insight into Marx's intellectual development. Their structure is unique and attests to their function in Marx's own internal critique of Hegel: he first reproduces the relevant paragraph from Hegel's book, and then sets down his criticism of it. It looks like and is a student's critical comment on his master's philosophy.

It is a deeply dialectical approach to Hegel: in each case Marx starts with accepting both Hegel's concepts as well as his system as a whole—and then subjects them to a critical confrontation with historical and contemporary reality. This is especially powerful in the way Marx confronts Hegel's concepts of property and civil society with existing reality.

A HEGELIAN RETROSPECTIVE

That the origins of Marx's socialism are in an internal radical critique of Hegel's philosophy is dramatically illustrated in an early contemporaneous article by Friedrich Engels, published in the *New Moral World*, an Owenite newspaper published in England, on 18th November 1843. Engels, a scion of a Rhenish Protestant industrialist family, became acquainted with the members of the Berlin Doktoren-Klub and met Marx for the first time in November 1842 at the editorial offices of the *RZ* in Cologne. His family had a business branch in Manchester and sent the young Engels there, where he established contacts with Robert Owen's socialist circles. Under the title "Progress of the Social Reform on the Continent," Engels reported to his English readers about the development of the various radical groups in France and Germany.

Writing about the beginnings of the socialist movement in Germany, Engels reported that there were two distinct German socialist groups or "parties"—one made up of working-class people and artisans, and the other "philosophical." First he described the working-class group and its most prominent leader, the tailor Wilhelm Weitling, and his work. Then he moved on to the "philosophical party," among whose members he named the poet Georg Herwegh and "Dr Ruge, Dr Marx, Dr Hess" (though Hess had never completed his academic education), re-

26

counting Marx's editorship at the *Rheinische Zeitung*. He claimed that the origins of this group lay in the development of German philosophy from Kant, Friedrich Schelling, and Fichte, culminating in Hegel's comprehensive system, "the like of which has never been seen before." He then elaborated:

> This system appeared quite unassailable from the without, and so it was; it has been overthrown from *within* only, by those who were Hegelians themselves. . . . Our party has to prove that either all the philosophical efforts of the German nation, from Kant to Hegel, have been useless—worse than useless; or that they must end in Communism; that the Germans must either reject their great philosophers, whose names they hold up to the glory of their nation, or that they must adopt Communism. And this *will* be proved . . .

This is obviously youthful bravado. Writing for a newspaper published in England, Engels felt unconstrained by any fear of censorship, and uses language that Marx would be careful to avoid in his own writings published under censorship conditions in Germany or France.

Many years later Marx did refer, albeit it in a cursory way, to how crucial the critical study of Hegel had been for his intellectual development. In the preface to his *Contribution to the Critique of Political Economy* in 1859—the first rough draft of what would eventually become *Das Kapital*—he wrote:

> The first work which I undertook to seek a solution to the doubts that assailed me was a critical review of the Hegelian philosophy of law [*Rechtsphilosophie*], a work the introduction to which appeared in 1844 in the *Deutsch-Französische Jahrbücher* [German-French Annals]. . . . My investigation led me to the conclusion that legal relations, such as forms of state, can be grasped neither only in themselves nor from the so-called general development of the human spirit, but rather have their roots in the material conditions of life, the sum

total of which Hegel, following the example of the Enlightenment and Frenchmen of the eighteenth century, combines under the name of "civil society" [*bürgerliche Gesellschaft*]; that, however, the anatomy of civil society is to be sought in political economy.

There is an interesting paradoxical admission in this statement: Marx admits that his road to a radical critique of existing society led through a theoretical critique of Hegel—not through a social analysis of actually existing conditions. But his account belittles the intensity with which he both internalized so much of Hegel's social terminology while going beyond it and in the process undermining the whole edifice of Hegelian political philosophy.

The reference to the short-lived journal *Deutsch-Französische Jahrbücher*, or *DFJ*, is revealing in more than one sense, as actually Marx contributed *two* essays to that collection. The second essay is titled "On the Jewish Question," and it too is deeply anchored in an internal critique of Hegel's political philosophy. But it also attests to Marx's complex relationship with Judaism and Jews and became later—and still is—an avatar for numerous debates and criticism. One can only speculate why in 1859 Marx did not even mention it.

There is, though, a further aspect to the titles Marx gave to these two essays in the *DFJ*. Both serve as the theoretical foundation for his call for a revolutionary overthrow of the existing social system by the proletariat: but nobody would guess this from the rather anodyne titles he gave to the essays—"Toward a Critique of Hegel's Philosophy of Right: An Introduction" and "On the Jewish Question." It is reasonable to assume that, by hiding his radical call for a revolutionary social and political transformation, Marx hoped to avert the eyes of customs and censorship officials; the collection was printed in Paris, with the intention of smuggling it across the Rhine into Germany. If this was the reason behind giving such quasi-academic titles to what were in fact revolutionary treatises, it failed: most of the copies were confiscated by Prussian customs officials, and only a few reached readers in Germany. For all the importance of the two essays to Marx's own intellectual development, they were hardly known at the time (although he did try, unsuccessfully, to republish them later).

THE PROLETARIAT—THE NEW UNIVERSAL CLASS

To understand how much Marx was indebted to Hegel's philosophy while radically transforming it, a quick glance at one of Hegel's distinct contributions to political philosophy is necessary.

In a nuanced and complex argument against the legacy of political and social philosophy from Thomas Hobbes, John Locke, and Adam Smith, Hegel argued in his *Philosophy of Right* that human relations cannot be subsumed under one dimension or consideration (self-interest, fear, or rational calculation); nor can they be explicated by an uncritical willingness to obey authorities legitimized by traditional allegiances, be they religious or dynastic. Instead he proposed a differentiated, multilayered system of allegiances, each motivated and legitimized by a distinct set of considerations. They are *family*, *civil society*, and *the state*. It is the balance among these allegiances that to Hegel characterizes the modern age.

In a somewhat schematic way one can characterize these three spheres of human relations as follows:

Family—particularistic altruism
Civil society—universal egoism
State—universal altruism.

The family—be it the modern nuclear family or the more traditional extended family or clan—is held together by the willingness of each member to act out of a feeling of altruism toward other persons, express solidarity with them, and be willing to do things out of these considerations. The family, according to Hegel, is not just a set of biological relations (obviously husband and wife are not biologically related), nor is it just a relationship of economic or sexual exchanges. The willingness of any member to work not just for himself but also for the benefit and welfare of others, the burden parents take upon themselves in providing for the sustenance and education of their children, the willingness of children to care for their parents in old age—all these cannot be viewed through considerations of maximizing one's own self-interest. However, this altruistic solidarity is limited within a prescribed circle of people, and hence its particularistic nature. While it may appear as an internal contradiction, it appears that altruism and particularism can go together, though their scope is obviously different in the case of a modern nuclear family compared with the more traditional, almost tribal families of pre-modern societies.

The family disintegrates precisely when this altruism and willingness to do things for the benefit of others ceases to function, and when some—or every—member of the family cares only for himself.

The dialectical antithesis to this altruistic particularism is universal egoism. This, to Hegel, is the sphere of civil society, where every member looks only for his self-interest: a grocer sells bread not because he cares for the welfare or health of his customers but because their needs are the vehicle he uses for his own profit; the financier is involved in his transactions not in order to enrich society but in order to enrich himself.

This is of course the opposite of the altruism of the family, and hence—this is an interesting Hegelian insight—the same person can be a loving husband or parent at home while being a ruthless and ferocious competitor in the marketplace; the two go together and even complement each other.

To regulate the marketplace, one needs general rules and laws: standard weights and measures, property laws, regulations about economic transactions, debt, and credit. This is the universal aspect of civil society—the need for objective general laws and their enforcement, enabling people to act in their own legitimate self-interest under well-established expectations. To Adam Smith's "invisible hand" Hegel adds the necessity for the regulatory functions of civil society.

The German term for civil society—*bürgerliche Gesellschaft*—grants a special deeper meaning to it, as it means not only *civil* society but also *bourgeois* society (something which later created some problems for English translators of Marx, as rendering it as mere "bourgeois society" detracts from its much richer connotations).

It is at this point that Hegel introduces his major contribution to modern political philosophy—and distances himself from the Hobbesian and Lockean tradition. He argues that anchoring the legitimacy of the state merely in individual self-interest of "life, liberty, and property" (or "the pursuit of happiness") misses the point. If this is the basis for the legitimacy of the state, why should people be forced to pay taxes, which in many cases means taking money from some people to cover the expenses of others? Moreover, what are the legitimacy and ethical justifications for the obligation to serve in the army and possibly jeopardize one's own limb and life in the process?

The conventional argument that people should pay taxes so that they can get public services—like policing or education—in return does not make sense, since some people, especially the rich, may claim that they can take better care of their interests on their own, yet it is not acceptable that they opt out of the public realm of the state. Similarly, and more dramatically, to argue that in serving in the army one defends himself and his family from the enemy is obvious nonsense: in terms of self-interest, the most rational thing for a person to do in a war situation is to get out of the country and take his family to a safer place and not endanger his life and possibly make his wife a widow and his children orphans.

The fact that this is not the way states operate suggests to Hegel that the attempt to legitimize the political realm—and the very existence of the state—by considerations of self-interest is a fallacy: such considerations are anchored in civil society, but do not operate in the political sphere. While it is legitimate to try to take out one's money if one's bank is about to go bankrupt, it is not considered legitimate to leave one's country when it is threatened by war; usually this is called treason.

It is for this reason that Hegel suggests that the legitimacy of the state lies somewhere else—in solidarity with one's fellow citizens, in what can be called universal altruism in the sense that it applies to all citizens of the polity. This is the political will to live in a community with other people, to be ready to bear burdens—financial or even existential—for the sake of this commonality; the state is a commonwealth, a *Gemeinwesen*, a *res publica* as against the *res privata* of civil society. It is more encompassing than either the family or civil society, but it does include these spheres within its wider scope. Hegel devotes considerable space in his *Philosophy of Right* to show how the two spheres of family and civil society should be integrated into the political realm.

Seen in this perspective, the state is in a way similar to the family in having altruism and solidarity at its core. But beyond the difference between the family's particularism and the state's universal norms, they are based according to Hegel on different foundations: the family's particularism is anchored in love, with its subjective ingredients, while the state is based on freedom and its objective institutions.

Out of this complex edifice Hegel developed his theory of social classes. He posits two kinds of social classes: on one hand are the traditional classes—peasants, the aristocracy, artisans, tradesmen, and merchants—each of whose members engages in their legitimate pursuit of their individual self-interests as members of civil/bourgeois society. But then Hegel adds a novel ingredient: the bureaucracy, which echoes the emergence in the early nineteenth century of a professional civil service in Napoleonic France (*carrière ouverte aux talents*) and then in the reformed Prussia of the 1810s and 1820s. This modern bureaucracy, according to Hegel, is on the one hand a class of civil society, but its actions are aimed at the *common* good: hence it should be guaranteed a fixed salary, and be recruited according to its merits, thus freeing it from worrying about its own interests in carrying out its duties in pursuing the policies of the commonwealth. Hence the bureaucracy to Hegel is both a class of civil society but also a "universal class," representing the general interests of the commonwealth.

While this is obviously a highly idealized vision of the bureaucracy, positing a class that is a vehicle of linking the individual self-interests of the various groups of civil society with the general good, it is Hegel's response to the transformation of the state from a patrimonial or semi-feudal structure to one responding to what he sees as the major characteristic of the modern state, with an independent bureaucracy balancing the various interests and ensuring that the state will not become a mere reflection of civil society interests.

As we have seen from Marx's articles in the *Rheinische Zeitung*, most of his critique of Prussian legislation and social and economic conditions questioned whether the modern state actually does represent the common interests—or is simply the expression of particular interests of the stronger groups in civil society. Later this analysis would lead him to brand the state as "nothing else than the executive committee of the ruling classes." To Marx this means that the Hegelian concept of the state as the guarantor of the common good is just a sham. These are the "doubts that had assailed" him that he mentioned in 1859: doubts about the veracity and adequacy of Hegel's political philosophy when compared to reality.

This is the underlying argument of Marx's *DFJ* essay "Toward a Critique of Hegel's Philosophy of Right: An Introduction." It culminates in a dialectical internal critique of Hegel's concept of a universal class: on the one hand he adopts this Hegelian concept, but he historicizes it. No longer is this concept limited to the role of the bureaucracy in the modern state: it becomes the foundation of Marx's first critical theory of social classes. In each historical epoch, he argues, there is a class that represents the overall interests of society at large, but it is a dynamic concept, whose bearers change from epoch to epoch. Rather than a fixed term related to modern bureaucracies, the Hegelian term of a universal class becomes for Marx an explicatory tool for the understanding of historical change and social hierarchy. Eventually it would lead him to what became the canonical opening sentence of *The Communist Manifesto*: "All history is the history of class struggle." Here is how Marx puts it in his essay on Hegel:

> No class in civil society can play this part unless it can arouse, in itself and in the masses, a moment of enthusiasm in which it associates and mingles with society at large, identifies itself with it, and is felt and recognized as the *general representative* of this society. Its aims and interests must genuinely be the aims and interests of society itself, of which it becomes in reality the social head and heart. It is only in the name of the general interest that a particular class can claim general supremacy . . . that genius which pushes material force to political power, that revolutionary daring which throws at its adversary the defiant phrase: *I am nothing and I should be Everything*.

The ringing echo in the closing sentence—referring to the statement of Abbé Sieyès during the French Revolution about what the Third Estate aspires to become—is a clear challenge to bourgeois claims to speak for all of society. Two years later, in a manuscript not published in his lifetime and eventually known as *The German Ideology*, Marx further elaborated his historization of the role of universal classes, now using a more explicit revolutionary language, this being after all a draft not aimed at publication at that stage.

> For each new class which puts itself in the place of one ruling before it, is compelled, merely in order to carry through its aims, to represent its interests as the common interests of all the members of society, that is, expressed in ideal form; it has to give its ideas the form of universality. . . . The class making a revolution appears from the very start . . . not as a class but as the representative of the whole of society.

In the *DFJ* essay Marx went on to maintain that historically all classes that claimed universality were overthrown sooner or later, because their claim to represent the general interests of all of society were either overtaken by social development or were a false pretense from the start. But now, he claims, there appears to be a class that is truly representative of all society— and it is in this context that Marx first mentions the proletariat; one cannot fail to notice how strongly, and how many times, Marx attributes to the proletariat the attributes of being a truly universal class.

> A class must be formed which has radical chains, a class of civil society which is not a class of civil society, a class which is the dissolution of *all* classes, a sphere of society which has a universal character because its sufferings are universal, and which does not claim a particular redress because the wrong done to it is not a particular wrong but wrong in general. There must be formed a sphere of society which claims no traditional status but only a *human* status, a sphere which is not opposed to particular consequences but is totally opposed to the assumptions of the German political system; a sphere,

finally, which cannot emancipate itself from all other spheres of society, without therefore emancipating all other spheres, which is, in short, a total loss of humanity which can only redeem itself by a total redemption of humanity. This dissolution of society as a particular class is the proletariat. [italics added]

This powerful passage in which the term "proletariat" first appears in Marx's writing is not in an economic or social analysis of its life conditions, but attributes to the proletariat the role of being the true universal class in the Hegelian sense, because its sufferings are universal. Continuing his claim for the historical redemptive role of the proletariat, Marx argues that dialectically, the proletariat in its present condition already incorporates in a negative fashion its positive message to humanity—the abolition of private property. In this way, when first mentioning the proletariat, Marx also clearly links it inextricably to the abolition of private property—that is, to communism.

When the proletariat announces the dissolution of the existing social order, it only declares the secret of its own existence, for it is the effective dissolution of this order. When the proletariat demands the abolition of private property it only lays down as a principle for society what society has already made the principle for the proletariat, and what the latter already involuntarily embodies as the negative result of society.

Marx ends his essay with a further embedding of the proletariat within the philosophical discourse by employing the Hegelian usage of the term *Aufhebung*. The nuances of this German word cannot be adequately rendered in translation, as it means both "keeping" and "raising to a higher level," but also "abolition." This complex meaning of the term in everyday German usage is employed by Hegel to signify the internal dialectics of development, when the realization of a concept also leads to its transcendence. In using this dialectical device, Marx suggests that on one hand the proletariat realizes, by its very existence, and eventual victory, the philosophical significance of being the true universal class, but this very fact also transcends philosophy by moving from theory to praxis, and thus abolishes philosophy itself as a separate sphere of activity because it will now be realized. Thus the emancipation of the proletariat—and with it of all society—is at the same time the actualization of philosophy as well as its transcendence and abolition.

> Philosophy is the head to this emancipation, and the proletariat is its heart. Philosophy can only be realized by the abolition [*Aufhebung*] of the proletariat, and the proletariat can only abolish itself [*sich aufheben*] by the realization of philosophy.

These philosophical undertones are also echoed in Marx's much later contention that the proletarian revolution will ultimately lead to the "abolition [*Aufhebung*] of the state": this is meant not just as an administrative abolition of state institutions but as a claim that, once the proletariat realizes the universal message of the state as representing universal norms and not particular interests, there is no need any more for a separate institution.

This ultimate relationship between theory and praxis is foreshadowed in the *DFJ* essay in what looks like a throwaway phrase but is obviously most central to Marx's argument about the link between philosophy and historical agency:

> The weapon of criticism cannot of course replace the criticism of weapons. Material force has to be overthrown by material force; but theory also becomes a material force when it takes hold of the masses.

Philosophy to Marx is not an academic disciple, but a vehicle for ultimate historical change, not—as he will state a bit later—just interpreting the world, but changing it. He starts with Hegel but then transcends him.

RELIGION AND OPIUM

Few of Marx's statements are as famous—and, of course, draw both great admiration and scathing criticism—as his assertion that "religion is the opium of the people." But few of those who quote it, whether approvingly or dismissively, are aware of the context in which it appears. And the context suggests that it is both more complex and more profound than its mere quotation as a staccato laconic judgment may suggest.

One of the aims of Marx's *DFJ* essay on Hegel's *Philosophy of Right* is his attempt to distance himself from the mainstream of the Young Hegelians, like Bruno Bauer, who had focused their writings on the critique of religion. Like many other Young Hegelians, Bauer came from a Protestant background, initially deeply anchored in theology: this, obviously, was not where Marx came from.

To Marx, a critique of religion misses the point both philosophically and socially. Marx agrees with Feuerbach that religion is a human construct ("man creates religion, religion does not create man"). Religious thought does indeed reflect human conditions, but according to Marx these have to be viewed in concrete historical contexts, not in the abstract.

> Religion is the self-consciousness and self-esteem of man who has either not yet found himself or has already lost himself again. But *man* is no abstract being situated outside the world. Man is *the world of man*, the state, society. This state, this society, produce religion, *an inverted world-consciousness*, because they are an inverted world.
>
> Religion is the general theory of this world, its encyclopedic compendium, its logic in a popular form . . . its moral sanction, its solemn complement, its universal source of con-

solation and justification. It is the *fantastic realization* of the human essence because the human essence has no true reality. The struggle against religion is therefore indirectly a struggle against the world of which religion is the spiritual *aroma*.

This historization of religious phenomena is the significant move from the critical theology of Feuerbach (and later, Søren Kierkegaard) to Marx's historically-anchored social criticism. Marx then concludes powerfully:

> Religious suffering is at the same time the *expression* of real suffering and also the *protest* against real suffering. Religion is the sigh of the oppressed creature, the heart of a heartless world, just as it is the spirit of a spiritless condition. It is the *opium* of the people.

Empathy, not scorn, for the suffering religious human being is what comes through very clearly here: religion is both the expression of human conditions of suffering but also a *protest* against them; it is not just a quietistic acceptance of quasi God-ordained suffering, but also a protest against this suffering. People seeking solace in religion are not just poor souls bamboozled by cynical ecclesiastical or political authorities: opium may not be the medicine that puts an end to pain, but it certainly alleviates it and has to be accepted and respected. At the same time, religious thinking is also a protest against inhuman conditions: "The criticism of religion is therefore in embryo the criticism of the vale of tears, of whose halo is religion. . . . The critique of heaven is the critique of earth."

The analogy to opium is telling and has methodological consequences: opium may alleviate pain, but it is not a cure. Similarly, a critique of religion, much as it may point to real suffering, does not and cannot be a solution to human suffering: this can only be found, not in a critique of religion, but in an action-oriented, transformative critique of "this state, society." Merely criticizing religion, without trying to identify the concrete social conditions that give rise to it, is to Marx shadow boxing, and unlike many other radicals, he finds it a waste of time. The battle has to be engaged against real social conditions, not against religion, which is just an expression of them. To use a later term of Marx, religion is part of the superstructure, and true radicalism has to go to the roots, to the social and economic infrastructure. This is the moment Marx parts company with the other Young Hegelians, whose trajectory continues to focus on a critique of religion: to Marx this is an exercise in futility. In a different and much more complex way, this is also his argument in the other *DFJ* essay, "On the Jewish Question," to which we turn now.

3

◆◈◆

"Zur Judenfrage"

MARX'S "ZUR JUDENFRAGE" [On the Jewish Question], published in 1844, is ostensibly a review and critique of Bruno Bauer's two tracts on Jewish emancipation that were published in the early 1840s. Yet it is a much more multilayered treatise, in which Marx not only argues against Bauer's views on Jewish emancipation, but also develops his own fundamental critique of the limits of the ideas and achievement of the French Revolution ("political emancipation") as against the more radical "human emancipation." Together with Marx's other *DFJ* essay, on Hegel's *Philosophy of Right*, this is the first presentation of his radical critique of Left Hegelianism, calling for a socialist revolution carried by the proletariat.

In his two essays, Bauer argued that so long as the Jews maintain their separate religion, they should not be granted equal rights. Basing his position on the Hegelian concept of the political realm, Bauer argues that the Jews cannot, on one hand, claim the universal right to participate in public affairs, and at the same time keep their particularistic identity as a religious community. Only if they give up their separateness and convert to Christianity, which is after all a universal religion, can they claim equal rights.

Marx finds this position unacceptable, and one cannot overlook that there is a passion in Marx's argument: it is obvious that he finds offensive Bauer's insistence on conversion as a condition for equal rights. As noted before, we do not know how much the circumstances of Heinrich Marx's conversion were discussed in the Marx household, but they obviously could not have been totally unknown, so Bauer's insistence on conversion—even if, after converting, Jews may transcend Christianity by adopting a universal critique of religion—did touch upon a personal level of experience, and it would be only natural that Marx could not remain totally oblivious of this.

The strong language of the first sentence of Marx's essay clearly suggests his more than purely theoretical engagement for Jewish emancipation and his insistence that the issue is political and not religious: "The German Jews desire emancipation. What kind of emancipation do they desire? Civic, political emancipation."

The multifaceted aspects of Marx's essay are also highlighted by its internal structure: the essay is presented by Marx in two distinct parts. Part 1 is a complex philosophical argument, steeped in Hegelian terminology, against Bauer's position, which denies the Jews *as they are* equal rights; here Marx develops his views of "human emancipation," which is a coded reference to social revolution, going beyond the mere political emancipation of the French Revolution. In this part Marx argues for equal rights for the Jews in the existing bourgeois society and harshly criticizes Bauer for excluding the Jews from society unless they convert: this, to Marx, is a proof that Bauer wasn't yet free from his Christian theological anti-Jewish prejudices and still viewed Judaism as an inferior religion. Marx's support for Jewish emancipation and equal rights is clear, and it is in this part that he describes the difference in the status of the Jews in different countries—in the German lands, in France, and in the United States. Referring to Alexis de Tocqueville's *Democracy in America*, he asserts that only in the United States, with its separation of state and religion, did the state fully emancipate itself from religion: at the same time, individuals are still deeply religious since, he argues, the alienation inherent in bourgeois society has not been overcome.

While Part 1 is a straightforward support for Jewish emancipation, Marx's essay became controversial, if not notorious, because of Part 2: this is where he expresses some extremely critical views about Judaism, identifying it with capitalism. It was this part that led some critics of Marxism during the Cold War to label Marx an anti-Semite or a "self-hating Jew," while making socialists, and especially Jewish socialists, extremely uncomfortable (a full Hebrew translation of "Zur Judenfrage" appeared only in 1965). The gap between the two parts of the essay may easily lead to a cognitive dissonance, on one hand, and misinterpretation on the other. This calls for a critical and nuanced reading of the totality of the two parts of the essay taken together.

Marx's argument in Part 1 of the essay is clear: the issue is one of political rights and is not a religious or theological question. He agrees with Bauer that current society is far from being fully free, but argues that the point is not the theological differences between Christianity and Judaism, but the rights of people who because of Christian triumphalism have been discriminated against and persecuted. Moreover, Bauer does not, according to Marx, distinguish between political emancipation, which entails among other things the separation of state and religion, and human emancipation, which will eventually liberate

43

all humankind from the very need for religion, which to Marx (as he stated in the essay on Hegel's *Philosophy of Right*) is "both the expression of real suffering and the protest against real suffering." To argue, as Bauer does, that Christians can be truly freed from religion by moving one step up, while Jews have to move two steps (embracing Christianity first), is a regression to theological scholasticism.

Most of Part 2 of "Zur Judenfrage" has a totally different tone. Here Marx launches an extreme and sometimes vituperative attack on Judaism. Had he published only Part 1 of his essay, he would be remembered as a champion of Jewish emancipation and equal rights; Part 2 has largely pushed the liberal political argument of Part 1 into the shadow and gained for Marx the reputation of a hater of Jews.

Part 2 opens with Marx reiterating his main argument against Bauer—that the issue is one of political rights, not of theology:

> Let us consider the real, worldly Jew [*den wirklichen, weltlichen Juden*], not the Sabbath Jew, as Bauer does, but the everyday Jew. Let us not look for the secret of the Jew in his religion, but let us look for the secret of his religion in the real Jews.

Such a sensible suggestion would appear to call either for an analysis of the role Jews play in contemporary society or of the way their real conditions of life are reflected in their religious beliefs and practices. But none of this follows. What follows is a rhetorically powerful onslaught on Judaism, totally devoid of any real social analysis of what Marx has just called "the everyday Jew," or of Jewish religious precepts. The lines are memorable for their staccato cadences:

> What is the secular [*weltlicher*] cult of the Jews? Huckstering [*Sacher*]. What is his secular God? Money ... What, in itself, was the basis of the Jewish religion? Practical need, egoism. The monotheism of the Jew, therefore, is in reality

the polytheism of the many needs, a polytheism which makes even the lavatory an object of divine law. Practical need, egoism, is the principle of civil society [*bürgerliche Gesellschaft*] . . .

Money is the jealous God of Israel, in the face of which no other God may exist. Money degrades all the Gods of man and turns them into commodities . . .

The God of the Jews has become secularized and has become the God of the real world. The bill of exchange is the real God of the Jew. His God is only an illusory bill of exchange . . .

The chimerical nationality [*Nationalität*] of the Jew is the nationality of the merchant, of the man of money in general.

The more one reads this vehement indictment, couched in almost biblical language, the more it becomes clear that Marx is writing about something beyond actual, living Jews. Despite his insistence that one should discuss "the everyday Jew," there is no reference to actually living Jewish people or their living conditions. Similarly, there is no mentioning of their religious practices—the reason, apparently, because Marx was totally ignorant of both, never having either experienced them directly or independently studied them. The only reference to any Jewish religious precept is the snide remark that Judaism has made "even the lavatory an object of divine law." This alludes to an obscure Jewish practice of thanking the Almighty after any ablution for supplying the human body with orifices, since otherwise human beings would perish. This is a thanksgiving prayer even most religious Jews may not be aware of; how did Marx come to know of it? A fair guess is he probably picked it up in the schoolyard of his Protestant humanistic *Gymnasium*.

Yet it is obvious that Marx is aiming at much more than "everyday Jews" when he goes on to write:

In North America the practical domination of Judaism over the Christian world has achieved its unambiguous and normal expression that the preaching of the gospel itself and the

Christian ministry have become articles of commerce and
the bankrupt businessman deals in the gospel just as the gospel preacher, who has become rich, goes for business deals.

Whatever one thinks of this passage, it is obvious that this is
not about Jews or Judaism: after all, there were very few Jews in
the United States at the time. It is, as he himself admits, about
the fact that "Money has become a world power [*Weltmacht*]."
Marx further maintains that it is the *Christian* world which is the
actual realization of what he has just identified with Judaism:

> Judaism reaches its highest point with the perfection of
> civil society, but it is only in the Christian world that civil
> society reaches its perfection. . . . Christianity sprang from
> Judaism. It has now been dissolved into Judaism.
>
> From the outset, the Christian was the theorizing Jew,
> the Jew is therefore the practical Christian, and the practical
> Christian has become a Jew again. Christianity has only in
> semblance overcome real Judaism. . . .
>
> Christianity is the sublime thought of Judaism. Judaism
> is the vulgar practical application of Christianity; but this
> application could only become general after Christianity as
> an accomplished religion had achieved theoretically the alien-
> ation of man from himself and from nature. Only then could
> Judaism achieve universal domination. . . .

If Marx's words on Judaism are harsh, his indictment of Christianity as the source of universal human alienation because of
the rule of money is even harsher.

Is Marx writing in code? Probably. When he ends Part 2 of
his essay with the resounding and—in retrospective, ominous—
words that "the social emancipation of the Jew is the emancipation of society from Judaism," his message is much wider: it is
about the emancipation of modern society from the power of
money, from capitalism (though he carefully avoids the term).
This is not to exculpate Marx or excuse him from the utterly un-

acceptable language he is using regarding Jews and Judaism: but he says similar things about Christianity in the modern world.

Given modern European history, Marx's language about Judaism is inexcusable. Yet the historical context in which he was writing should not be overlooked.

The first point is that if Marx was writing in code, the code was known and understood by his contemporaries. In German parlance of the time, *Judentum* also stood for commerce, trade, huckstering in general, just as the English verb "to jew" (now excised from the Oxford English Dictionary) used to mean "to cheat." So when Marx says that American society is the apotheosis of the power of "Judaism" or that society should be emancipated from the thrall of "Judaism," there is a subtext here: contemporary readers would recognize that he was not writing just about Jews. Fear of censorship might also have convinced Marx to use the colloquial *Judentum* rather than "capitalism."

Second, and ironically, Marx's identification of Judaism with capitalism has a paradoxical literary origin. It appears for the first time in Germany in an article by Marx's socialist colleague Moses Hess called "On Money" [Über das Geldwesen], which was published a year later but, as has been clearly established, Marx had read in manuscript form *before* writing his own essay. Unlike Marx, who as his own essay shows was quite ignorant of all matters Jewish, Hess, who never converted to Christianity, went to a religious Jewish school, knew Hebrew, and was conversant in Jewish religious practices. In his article Hess identifies Judaism historically with money and a money-based culture; he even speculates—through a highly spurious etymological analysis of the Hebrew words for blood (*dam*) and money (*damim*)—that Judaism was initially connected to human sacrifices, which were later converted into cash penalties. Blissfully, Marx did not adopt this nonsense, but basically follows Hess's identification of Judaism with money. Yet there is a deeper irony here: many years later, in 1862, in *Rom und Jerusalem: Die lettzte Nationalitäten Frage* [Rome and Jerusalem: The Last Nationality Question], Hess called for the establishment of a Jewish commonwealth in Palestine and became one of the forerunners of modern Zionism. Hess's intellectual journey is another example of the convoluted and tortuous route of many Jewish nineteenth-century intellectuals in the age of both emancipation and rising nationalism.

Yet the enormous gap between the two parts of Marx's essay still raises a number of troubling questions. After all, the theoretical and political thrust of the essay is in Part 1, where Marx supports Jewish emancipation and attacks Bauer for his demand that Jews convert before being granted equal rights. Why, after such a spirited defense, would Marx then launch into a far-reaching attack on Judaism? True, as one learns even from Thomas Macaulay's *On the Civil Disabilities of the Jews in Britain*, a classical liberal argument from 1833 supporting equal rights for Jews, one does not have to particularly like Jews or Judaism in order to support their equal rights as citizens. Yet the rhetoric of Marx in Part 2 is laced with so much hyperbole and venom that it gives cause to pause and wonder.

One cannot find a satisfying answer to these questions from Marx's own writings, manuscripts, or correspondence. But perhaps one can speculate: because the argument followed by Marx in Part 1 for equal rights is so powerful, he might have felt that he had to bend over backward and distance himself as much as possible from Jews and Judaism so as not to be accused of supporting Jewish rights because of his own Jewish background. Perhaps the echoes of his own family's conversion to Christianity due to discriminatory views and Christian prejudices, as expressed by Bauer, were so strongly reverberating in Marx's consciousness that he defensively sought to dissociate himself from even a whiff of lingering identification with Judaism, to prove that his anti-Bauer argument was unrelated to his family's background.

In other words: is the tension between the two parts of "Zur Judenfrage" an expression of some *Zerrissenheit*, or inner turmoil, in Marx's own consciousness, of a Faustian innermost struggle so memorably expressed by Goethe:

> Two souls, alas, dwell in my breast,
> And each seeks to break away from the other.
> [Zwei Seelen wohnen, ach, in meiner Brust,
> Die eine will sich von der andern trennen.]

We may never know, nor is it possible to reconstruct Marx's own views on the complex circumstances of his father's conversion. Was there anger, or even shame, connected with it? Perhaps in writing as he did, he was exhibiting not only the two souls dwelling within his breast but also expressing, in a painful and convoluted way, two burdens: that of his Jewish background as well as that of his family's conversion to Christianity, which lacked any spiritual or religious conviction but was ultimately motivated by purely professional if not pecuniary considerations. We do not know, but it would be wrong to divorce the complexity of Marx's arguments in his essay from his own family history, despite the fact that it was never acknowledged publicly.

ANOTHER DEFENSE OF JEWISH EMANCIPATION

There is, however, a sequel to the essay "Zur Judenfrage," yet it is mostly overlooked, even though it may supply a further insight into Marx's inner tensions connected with his Jewish background. He came back to the issue in this slightly later work, *Die heilige Familie* [The Holy Family], written together with Friedrich Engels and published in 1845. That this book has been generally ignored should not be surprising, as it is not one of the best written works by Marx and Engels: it is a lengthy, tedious, and pedantic criticism of various Young Hegelians, basically an in-family polemic where esoteric arguments about minor and petty differences are raised to world-historical dimensions. Among the thinkers subjected to what is sometimes acerbic yet highly scholastic petty criticism in its three hundred pages of disjointed essays are Bruno Bauer, his brother Edgar Bauer, Max Stirner, and others. The volume may have been extremely significant for Marx and Engels in distancing themselves from other Young Hegelians, yet most of it is rightly forgotten.

For our purposes, however, some of it is meaningful. Three sections of Chapter 6 are each titled "Zur Judenfrage"; the volume's original table of contents identifies which of the two authors wrote each section, and all three of these sections are explicitly attributed to Marx.

Marx opens by referring to two further articles by Bauer published in the *Allgemeine Literatur-Zeitung*, in which he responded to some Jewish writers who reacted to his initial essays on the Jewish question.

Each of Marx's three sections is actually a short independent essay, and two aspects stand out: first of all, the extreme criticism of Judaism in Part 2 of "Zur Judenfrage" is totally absent and is not repeated; second, Marx refers approvingly, and in some detail, to a number of Jewish polemicists against Bauer (Gustav Philippson, Samuel Hirsch, Gabriel Riesser). In each case Marx supports their views and calls them "liberal and rationalist Jews." Already living at that time in exile in Paris, and having become acquainted with French conditions, Marx widens the scope of his argument to include references to the Jews in France. He goes out of his way to support positions taken by the French Jewish leader Adolphe Crémieux, the founder of the Alliance Israelite Universelle, one of the first modern, transborder Jewish organizations.

Marx's general argument here against Bauer and in support of Jewish emancipation follows the line he took in Part 1 of his original essay: that Bauer's exclusion of Jews from civic rights and equal citizenship reflects traditional Christian theological anti-Judaism. Marx quotes approvingly Philippson's contention that Bauer projects an "ideal philosophical state," overlooking the fact that the question of Jewish civic rights has to be approached in the context of existing society; and given its principles there can be no argument against granting the Jews equal rights.

Marx then describes in some detail the acrimonious debate between Bauer and the Dessau rabbi Samuel Hirsch. When Hirsch, in a typical Jewish apologetic argument, maintained that after all, the Jews did contribute something to history and "modern times," Bauer dismisses this by apparently agreeing but then adding that the Jews have always been "an eyesore" to Christian society. Marx's response to this is vehement, as if he has been personally offended:

> Something that has been an eyesore to me from birth, as the Jews have been to the Christian world, and which persists and develops with the eye is not an ordinary sore, but a wonderful one, one that really belongs to my eye and must even contribute to a highly original development of my eyesight. . . . [This] revealed to Herr Bruno [Bauer] the significance of Jews in "the making of the modern times."

Marx then supports the position of Gabriel Riesser—the most outspoken Jewish proponent of emancipation—in his polemic against Bauer.

> Mr Riesser correctly expresses the meaning of the Jews' desire for recognition of their free humanity when he demands, among other things, the freedom of movement, sojourn, travel, earning one's living, etc. These manifestations of "free humanity" are explicitly recognized in the French Declaration of the Rights of Man.

Perhaps one should not read too much into the reference to the right "of earning one's living," and connecting this to the French Declaration of the Rights of Man, under which Jews in France (and in French-controlled Rhineland) were emancipated—the precise context of his own father's conversion after the post-

1815 revocation of these rights. This may, however, be the only reference—oblique as it is—to his family history and what must have been a humiliating memory.

Marx provides a wider dimension to the question of Jewish emancipation when he refers to a debate in the French Chamber of Deputies, when Deputy Adolphe Crémieux declared that French Jews should accept the public observance of Sunday as an official day of rest "out of respect for the religion of the majority of Frenchmen." But then Marx adds a surprisingly critical note, bringing out the dilemmas of Jews even in a liberal state that grants them equal rights. This is how he puts it:

> Now according to free theory, Jews and Christians are equal, but in practice Christians have a privilege over Jews; for otherwise how could the Sunday of the Christians have a place in a law made for all Frenchmen? Should not the Jewish Sabbath have the same rights?

It is perhaps ironic that after having written what he did in his original essay about Judaism, Marx comes out here, even if only for the sake of argument, in defense of the Jewish Sabbath. Yet it is clear to him that while Jews should have equal rights in existing society, the French case suggests how even in relatively liberal societies, full equality can be achieved: only in a state of "human emancipation," which would transcend the alienation inherent in bourgeois society, only when no religious creed—neither Christian nor Jewish—would be necessary anymore to give solace to human suffering.

Summing up his position *contra* Bauer, Marx states unequivocally that "the Jew who demands freedom and nonetheless is not willing to give up his religion . . . is making a demand which does not contradict political freedom." This is quite an extraordinary argument made by Marx, calling for respect for Jewish religious cultural self-determination.

Moreover: the civic status of the Jews becomes for Marx a

criterion by which to judge a country's general politics: "The states which cannot yet emancipate the Jews politically have to be judged against the fully developed political states—and found wanting."

It is not totally clear why Marx found it necessary to revisit in such great detail his polemic against Bauer on Jewish emancipation, and devote to it three separate sections of *Die heilige Familie*, quoting so extensively and supportively Jewish polemicists against Bauer. The very fact that he followed the writings of Bauer's Jewish critics and was familiar with their arguments suggests that the issue remained important to him. Was he perhaps a bit uneasy about the way his extreme attacks on Judaism in Part 2 of his initial "Zur Judenfrage" could be misconstrued and used against granting Jews full equal rights and thus undermine his own support for Jewish emancipation? Did he feel that his equation of *Judentum* with modern capitalism was misguided? Did he want—now living in France—to distance himself from French socialists, like Charles Fourier and some of his disciples, who viewed French Jewish bankers and financiers as the symbols of capitalism? There is no clear answer to these questions. Yet the extensive discourse in *Die heilige Familie* clearly shows the double dimension of Marx's views on the issue: a radical critique of Judaism (and, incidentally, of Christianity) as a religion, coupled with unequivocal support for civic equality for Jews and their right to retain their religion without having to convert in order to enjoy equal rights and full citizenship.

Marx followed this theoretical position during the revolutionary atmosphere of 1848, when serving as editor of the *Neue Rheinische Zeitung*. He reported about a delegation of Jewish leaders from Cologne who came to ask for his support for granting full equal rights to the Jews. As in his theoretical writings, his response was indicative of his separating his views about Judaism from his support for Jewish emancipation: in a letter to Arnold Ruge he says that he will of course support the Jewish leaders' petition for equal rights out of political principle, despite the fact that "their religion has always been distasteful [*widerlich*] to me."

A few years later, Marx took a similar position when discussing the election of the first Jewish member to the British parliament in 1853. The banker Lionel Rothschild was elected to the House of Commons for the City of London but could not take his seat, because incoming MPs were required to take a Christian oath on entering office. In a newspaper article Marx did not miss the opportunity to refer to Rothschild as a usurer, but concluded that it would be "an absolute absurdity" to deny him his seat because of his Jewishness "after the spirit of usury has so long presided in the British Parliament."

Marx's journalistic writings also reflect his theoretical position on the relationship between Jewish emancipation and the modern liberal state. When in late 1848 the achievements of the first heady months of the revolution in Germany were slowly being reversed, Marx twice commented in the *NRZ* that one indication that reactionary power was reasserting itself was the abolition of steps leading to Jewish emancipation and equal citizenship rights: such steps were a clear sign that the revolutionary liberal wave was on its way out. As in his earlier essays, Jewish equal rights are a criterion by which the modern state has to be judged.

As for Bruno Bauer, in 1863 he published a violent anti-Jewish tract called *Das Judentum in der Fremde*, arguing how alien Judaism was to the German spirit; in his later years he became a supporter of Bismarckian policies and a spokesman for German expansionist nationalism.

4

Paris and Brussels: Formative Years

THAT THE YOUNG MARX made an enormous impression on his contemporaries is reflected in an unusually adulatory letter written by Moses Hess in 1841 to another Rhenish Jewish author, Berthold (Baruch) Auerbach. In 1837, Auerbach had published the first modern German biography of Spinoza, who came to symbolize for many emancipated and educated Jews the idea that one could be a member of the European republic of letters while still retaining one's Jewish identity, albeit in a critical way. Hess was several years Marx's senior; he had already published two philosophical books advocating communism (*The Holy History of Mankind* and *The European Triarchy*), and it was he who had introduced Marx to some of the Rhenish radicals in Bonn and Cologne. So his willingness to defer to what he saw as Marx's genius was not empty praise. After reporting about some personal matters, Hess advised Auerbach on 2nd September 1841:

> Be prepared to meet the greatest, perhaps the only real philosopher living now. When he will appear in public (both in his writings as well as at the university), he will draw the eyes of all Germany upon him. . . . He goes beyond Strauss and even beyond Feuerbach. . . . Such a man I always wanted to have as my teacher in philosophy. Only now do I feel what an idiot in philosophy I have been . . .
>
> Dr Marx—this is the name of my idol—is still a young man, barely 24 years old, but he will give the final blow to all medieval religion and politics; he combines the deepest philosophical seriousness with a cutting wit. Can you imagine Rousseau, Voltaire, Holbach, Lessing, Heine, and Hegel combined—not thrown together—in one person? If you can—you have Dr Marx.

The academic career was not to be, and the trajectory of Marx's life took a different turn; yet Marx's writings did indeed eventually "draw the eyes" not only of "all Germany" on him.

Yet the singularity of Marx's intellectual brilliance and learning also carried a hidden curse that accompanied him for most of his life: because he was so intellectually superior to many of his colleagues in the socialist movement, he could not stop himself from pointing out the inconsistencies in their writings, their occasional muddled thoughts, and sometimes their sheer ignorance. As a consequence, many of his polemical writings were aimed, harshly and unsparingly, at his comrades-in-arms. This made Marx a brilliant polemicist, but not exactly a pleasant or accommodating member in a movement where solidarity and collegiality were crucial. Not only Bruno Bauer and other Young Hegelians, but also Moses Hess himself, as well as Proudhon, Arnold Ruge, Bakunin, and many, many others found themselves victims of Marx's acid tongue and acerbic intellectual wit. Not taking prisoners was a signature of Marx's writings, and it certainly did not endear him to his closest colleagues, whom he consistently made into his enemies. This trait followed him most of his life: he was perhaps his own worst enemy, and therefore he had little impact on social and political developments during his lifetime. Posthumously, of course, things would develop differently, mainly thanks to the unwavering efforts of Engels.

The 1840s were not only Marx's most productive years, but also his most formative ones. Through extensive reading, processed through his critical mind, he was able to form his own theories, in many cases through harsh criticism of some of his closest friends and colleagues.

After leaving Germany in October 1843, Marx lived in Paris among the growing German community of radical exiles. His activities were monitored by the Prussian authorities, who succeeded in convincing the French government to expel him in February 1845. He moved to Brussels, where he lived until the revolutions of 1848 upended European politics and his own life. Before leaving Paris, he hastily penned a goodbye note to Heinrich Heine—the doyen of German radical exiles in the French capital—saying that, of all he was being forced to leave behind in the city, Heine was the dearest and most cherished.

Yet as an exile in Brussels, Marx's position remained precarious. He had to petition the Belgian authorities for a residence permit, and was granted one only after formally signing a document pledging "on my word of honor not to publish in Belgium any work on current politics." Marx constantly felt that he might be expelled from Belgium as well, and his fears led him even to consider emigrating to the United States. In the summer and autumn of 1845 he started making enquiries in this direction and tried to obtain the necessary documents required, including a certificate confirming his medical exemption from Prussian military service. Nothing came of these attempts, and after the initial uncertainties it appears that Marx found Brussels a relatively safe haven—although one may be tempted to speculate about the possible consequences if Marx had spent the rest of his life in America.

Both in Paris and in Brussels his life ran on two parallel though connected levels: on one hand, he was involved with a whole range of radical associations and groups, which drew the attention of the political police both in Belgium and in his native Prussia, but whose impact on political and social developments was minimal. But as part of this association, Marx, the perennial student and intellectual, worked hard to clarify his own thoughts, and this intellectual effort—part of which was published at the time, but most was confined to manuscript notes published only later, in some cases decades after his death—is a testimony to the breadth of his knowledge and the complex trajectory of his intellectual development. It was also at that time that his family grew step by step: in May 1844 his first daughter, Jenny, was born in Paris; after having moved to Brussels, his second daughter, Laura, was born in September 1845; in December 1846 his son Edgar was born.

Not having any fixed employment or source of income during these years, Marx's financial situation was obviously precarious. He was occasionally paid for some of his articles, and in July 1845 a radical publisher in Darmstadt advanced him 1,500 francs on account of a planned book on politics and political economy (which was never delivered, despite extensive preparatory studies). But in many cases he depended on family funds—some through his wife's dowry, in many cases through unpleasant haggling with his tightfisted mother. Brothers-in-law in Maastricht lent him 150 francs in September 1847, but only in February 1848 did he succeed in getting a settlement of 6,000 francs of inheritance from his father. This was a significant sum at the time, but continuing financial squabbles with his mother followed him for many years.

Intellectually and politically the years in Paris were indeed

a turning point for Marx; after the Bourbon dynasty was replaced in 1830 by the Orleanists, a more liberal France became
the refuge for radicals from all over Europe. German artisans
and workers as well as Italian and Russian revolutionaries found
asylum in the French capital, where the revolutionary traditions had not been totally eradicated during the post-1815 Restoration. It was here that Marx met Heinrich Heine and other
democratic and radical exiles, and it was from Paris that Marx and
his Young Hegelian colleague Arnold Ruge launched the *DFJ*.

It was in Paris that Marx became better acquainted with
the Saint-Simonians, and also met the French socialists Pierre-
Joseph Proudhon, Louis Blanc, and Pierre Leroux, as well as the
legendary Russian revolutionary Mikhail Bakunin, with whom
he became extremely close.

It was also in these years that Marx began his close association with Friedrich Engels, who became the lifelong collaborator and friend of Marx, who usually managed to quarrel with
most of his closest colleagues. They came from different backgrounds and were personally as far apart as possible: Marx the
intellectual and philosopher, Engels the down-to-earth industrialist and brash man of affairs; one with a complicated Jewish
background, the other from a Lutheran self-assured family; one
was drawn to socialism through his philosophical studies, the
other through his day-to-day contact with the working class in
Manchester. Yet their bond was deep and lasting, and it was
Engels who for many years helped to keep the Marx family
above water during the first difficult years in London after 1849,
and continued to support Marx also after his financial situation
got more secure. Engels deferred to Marx's intellectual brilliance
and superiority, and Marx always acknowledged his enormous
debt to the crucial support of his rich friend. In the annals of
political and intellectual partnership, it was indeed a unique relationship, though the differences in some aspects of their ap-

proach to politics and history cannot be overlooked: Marx came from the humanities, Engels from practical economic activity, with a lasting interest in natural sciences.

Engels occasionally traveled from Manchester to Paris (and later to Brussels), and the two began their collaboration in writing during these visits. It was mainly through Engels's book *The Condition of the Working Class in England*, published in 1845, that Marx became better acquainted with the real-life conditions of the industrial workers, helping him to move from the somewhat abstract philosophical endorsement of the proletariat as the "universal class" in the *DFJ* essay on Hegel to a concrete social analysis of the actual working class.

The literary production of Marx in the Paris and Brussels years was prodigious. He and Engels published *The Holy Family* in 1845, and then they continued their criticism of the Young Hegelians in what was later called *The German Ideology*, although this book was never published at the time. Decades later Engels justified the fact that the book had not been published by arguing that the 1848 revolution upset their life and plans, and that in any case these pages merely helped to clarify their own thoughts, so they both were happy to leave them "to the gnawing criticism of the mice." In 1847 Marx published in French his critique of Proudhon, *The Poverty of Philosophy*, but his most extensive work, the *Economic-Philosophical Manuscripts*, written in 1844, did not see the light until the late 1920s, and was not fully published in a critical edition until after World War II. An accompanying short manuscript, the seminal *Theses on Feuerbach*, was similarly published only posthumously by Engels in the 1880s. Besides these works, Marx wrote numerous articles for various radical newspapers (*Vorwärts* in Paris and then the *Deutsche Brüsseler Zeitung*). Toward the end of 1847, again with Engels and with some help from Hess, Marx prepared *The Communist Manifesto*.

This is a lot, but it is a mixed bag. Some of it is focusing on obscure and mostly irrelevant polemics with long forgotten Young Hegelians, and bears out Engels's comment about a well-deserved gnawing criticism of the mice. But among the jejune in-house polemics against erstwhile colleagues, one can find gems of thought-provoking and original ideas. Some of these pieces are justly viewed as part of the core of Marx's theories of history and society—even though, as in the case of the *Economic-Philosophical Manuscripts* or the *Theses on Feuerbach*, they were not published in his lifetime but provide the building blocks of some of his later ideas.

Most of Marx's writing in this period, both published as well as manuscript notes, is devoted to distancing his thought from his former Young Hegelian colleagues. His main argument against them is that they remain stuck in philosophical and theological matters, while he—as he mentioned later in the *Introduction to the Critique of Political Economy* from 1859—had moved, through an internal critique of Hegel, to the understanding that one has to relate to real social conditions and not just to their reflection in intellectual discourse.

The very title *The Holy Family—or the Critique of Critical Critique* drips with heavy-handed irony. Its disdain for the Christian concept of a "holy family" is also aimed at the Bauer family—Bruno and Edgar Bauer, who established themselves as the mainstay of the Young Hegelian school—and the wordplay on the term "critique" highlighted what to Marx was their sham radicalism, which to him meant that they never transcended the world of philosophy, theology, and literary criticism. The agenda of the book is pithily encapsulated in its opening paragraph, written in somewhat carefully crafted coded language, as Marx and Engels hoped their book, published in Germany, would somehow avoid the eyes of the censors:

> Real *humanism* has no more dangerous enemy in Germany than *spiritualism* or *speculative idealism*, which substitutes *"self-consciousness"* or the *"spirit"* for the *real individual man*.

The italics in the original give the game away: the point is to go beyond the spiritual to the material, real conditions—and for that reason the book goes with a fine comb through the writings of the "spiritual" or "speculative" Young Hegelians, suggesting that their writings are irrelevant as a critique of real life: they are only criticizing criticism, not life.

We have already seen how Marx used this tool in dismantling Bruno Bauer's argument that the way for Jews to gain equal rights is first of all to convert. It was not the real-life conditions of the Jews or their civil and political rights in the here-and-now that concerned Bauer, but their faith: this is an argument out of theology, not real life—and hence, according to Marx, irrelevant.

Going beyond the controversy with Bauer and his colleagues, Marx devotes a lengthy section of Chapter 6 to comments on the French Revolution and its Jacobin phase. It is interesting because both some German radicals—and certainly the French republican tradition—have viewed the Jacobin leaders Maximilien Robespierre and Louis de Saint-Just as a possible model for a future radical revolution, even applauding the Reign of Terror (Lenin and his followers did the same). In a surprising critique of the Jacobins, Marx argues that the Reign of Terror was itself a testimony of the failure of Jacobin politics because of their wrongheaded fascination with classical Rome, encapsulated in Saint-Just's call to "Let revolutionary men be Romans" or his nostalgic complaint that, since the Romans, "the world is a void, and only their memory fills it and prophesizes liberty."

This to Marx is not only empty romanticism but would also be responsible for the Jacobins' shift toward terrorism: the Roman republican tradition focused exclusively on political arrangements in the state, whereas modern societies have to grapple with the tension between civil, bourgeois society and the political realm—an issue totally unknown in Roman history. The tragedy of the Jacobins—and those in Germany and France who have not learned from their failure—was that because they tried to impose quasi-Roman solutions on a modern society with its modern class structure, they drifted toward terrorism in a futile attempt to force their historical model on a totally different society, which proved utterly recalcitrant to being molded according to the Roman example.

This criticism of Jacobin terrorism is both intellectually and politically of high significance, and would accompany Marx all his life. As we shall see in his programmatic sections of *The Communist Manifesto*, Marx believed that social developments and economic transformations would lead to a different society, transcending the class struggles of capitalism; but any attempt to use force when conditions are not ripe for internal change are doomed to the tragedy—and cruelty—of the Jacobin terror. To Marx the failure of the Jacobins was inherent in their ahistorical approach: to craft an eighteenth- or nineteenth-century society according to a Roman model of the first century B.C. is irresponsible, dangerous, and doomed to failure and bloodshed. Some people and movements who maintained that they were following Marx's revolutionary prescriptions fatally overlooked his strictures against the futility and dangers—moral and political—of revolutionary terrorism.

HOMO FABER AND ALIENATION: THE FOUNDATIONS OF PHILOSOPHICAL ANTHROPOLOGY

Marx's most significant corpus of writing from the Paris period was never published in his lifetime, nor was it meant to be: this was the so-called *Economic-Philosophical Manuscripts* of 1844. Like the Kreuznach critique of Hegel's *Philosophy of Right*, the manuscripts were aimed at clarifying Marx's own thoughts, partially through a meticulous critical reading of texts by other authors. Few nineteenth-century revolutionary thinkers paid similar attention to reading other people's writings: this method gave extraordinary depth to Marx's writing, but also much delayed his ability to arrive at final, publishable conclusions.

The notebooks of the *Economic-Philosophical Manuscripts* (*EPM*) are very different in form and content from one another: some, especially those dealing with economic issues, are straightforward summaries of books by various economists; others present Marx's own thoughts on the role of labor as the foundation of human existence and the sources of human history; some are dry economic accounts, while others provide dramatic descriptions of the alienation of the worker in modern industrial society; finally, some lead to almost poetical visions of the redemptive promises of communism. All of this is accompanied by another critique of Hegel's thought and especially his dialectics.

These basically reading notes and sketches are prefaced, however, by a programmatic introduction, which is actually the mission statement of Marx's life project—of the magnum opus he never really managed to finish and of which *Das Kapital* would ultimately be supposed to be merely the first volume.

> I have already announced in the *Deutsch-Französische Jahrbücher* the critique of jurisprudence and political science in the form of a critique of Hegel's *Philosophy of Right*. . . . Now I will try to point out the overall connections . . . between political economy and the state, the law, morality, civil life etc. . . . It is hardly necessary to assure the reader that I have reached my conclusions by means of a wholly empirical analysis based on a conscientious critical study of political economy.

This is obviously a highly ambitious task, and Marx is well aware of the fact that it has to be based on an extensive study of the whole corpus of economic writing—which he does in the first three manuscripts, which deal with labor, capital, and land rent (issues that appear again later, in a slightly different order, in *Das Kapital*). At the same time Marx notes his indebtedness to French and English socialists, and also points out what he calls "the seminal writings" of Moses Hess on socialism and communism and his essay "The Philosophy of the Deed" [Die Philosophie der Tat], which focuses on the active ingredient in radical philosophy, going beyond the speculative writings of the Young Hegelians.

The economic parts of the *EPM*, with their detailed analysis, especially of Adam Smith, are less interesting and original than what follows next, however—Marx's first development of his philosophical anthropology.

In a section called "Alienated Labor," Marx sets out in dramatic and crystalline language his views of the specificity of human being (*Gattungswesen*): man to Marx is not *Homo sapiens*, but primarily *Homo faber*, the creative being who has a unique dialectical relationship to nature and to the objective world, which both sustains him and is also formed by his labor and his activity. This human activity constantly changes both nature and man himself.

To Marx the major difference between humans and other animals is that animals are sustained by the means that nature puts at their disposal and are therefore constrained and limited by what nature offers them as food or shelter: their relationship to nature is basically passive, constant, and limited to their biological determination. Humans, on the other hand, shape nature, change it, and mold it to their need; in doing this, they also create new needs, whereas the needs of other animals are unchanged and strictly determined biologically. By creating new needs, humans also create history—as history is the developmental way by which they supply their needs through labor. Labor obviously needs a material, natural foundation, but it is changing nature, whereas animals just take from nature what it offers and leave it as it is. Without naming it "historical materialism," this is the crux of Marx's philosophical anthropology: labor is thus the foundation of human active consciousness: before being *Homo sapiens,* man is *Homo faber.*

As becomes also clear from Marx's straightforward description, he himself was losing the fetters of the speculative language he inherited from the Hegelian tradition:

> Of course, animals also produce. They construct nests, dwellings, as in the case of bees, beavers, ants, etc. But they only produce what is strictly necessary for themselves or their young. They produce only in a single direction, while man produces universally. They produce only under the compulsion of direct physical need, while man produces when he is free from physical needs and only truly produces in freedom from such needs.

Humans' labor enables them to transcend mere needs, which means they are not slaves to their needs: labor is not bondage, but constitutes real freedom and their essence as a species.

Moreover, Marx argues that by processing nature and changing the natural object through labor, humans create external objects that stand apart from them—very different from what one sees in animals. Humans are also not limited to one method of relating to nature. Marx's language borders on the poetic, without losing its empirical basis:

> The products of animal production belong directly to their physical bodies, while man is free in face of his product. Animals construct only in accordance with the standards and needs of the species to which they belong, while man knows how to produce in accordance with the standards of every species and knows how to apply the appropriate standard to the object. Hence man can produce also in accordance with the laws of beauty.

This humanistic basis of Marx's philosophical anthropology serves as the foundation of his criticism of bourgeois society and modern capitalism. He shares the general criticism of other socialists who view capitalism as unjust and exploitative, yet he does not stop at this moralistic critique, which can be countered by arguing that every moral statement is itself a historically anchored social construct. Marx's critique of capitalism goes further: industrial capitalism is not just oppressive; it basically dehumanizes every worker in a most fundamental way, by depriving them of their basic humanity, which is embedded in their being *Homo faber*, the creator of themselves and of human history.

This historical contextualization of the role of the worker in capitalist society singles out Marx's critique of capitalism and thus transcends mere moralism. Marx is of course aware that all previous modes of production were exploitative: but it is only in modern industrial capitalism that the producer is totally divorced both from his product and from his own role as producer.

This is Marx's theory of alienation, and here again he uses a Hegelian term (*Entfremdung*) but changes it totally: in the Hegelian tradition, alienation is a state of mind, of consciousness, which can be overcome by a change in consciousness. To Marx, the alienation of the worker results in total dehumanization: modern workers are alienated from the product of their work, from the process of production that is now mediated through machines, from their role as the creator of the actual human world through their labor—and from their own humanity. Only if one sees the essence of human beings in their role as *Homo faber* can one reach such a radical critique of what capitalism does to the modern proletariat.

The point for Marx is that in previous modes of production, medieval artisans or peasants did after all retain at least part of the product of their labor; in modern capitalism, the workers do not retain any part of what they produce—all they get is a wage, which is just a means to enable them to survive. Not only do they not own even a fraction of what they produce, but the modern division of labor even deprives them of viewing the end product of their labor as something that is part of themselves— something the traditional artisans or even peasants could claim and be, in a way, even proud of what they had produced. The modern workers have no relationship to their product; they are just a means for the capitalist's ability to gain a profit. Nor are the workers' wages related in any way to the value of what they have produced. Under capitalism, labor, which is the essence of human beings, diminishes them.

> What constitutes the alienation of the worker? First, that labor is external to the worker, it does not belong to his intrinsic nature, that in his work he does not affirm himself but denies himself . . . does not develop freely his physical and mental energy but mortifies his body and ruins his mind. The worker feels at home only outside his work. . . . His labor is therefore not voluntary but coerced. . . . It is therefore not the satisfaction of need, it is merely a means to satisfy needs external to it.

In other words, what is the human's essence—labor—becomes a mere instrument for other needs. Moreover,

> Man (the worker) feels himself freely active only in his animal functions—eating, drinking, procreating . . . and in his human functions he no longer feels himself to be anything but an animal. What is animal-like becomes human and what is human becomes animal-like.

Although Marx never studied directly the life condition of the modern proletariat, he refers to descriptions found in the writings of French socialists, and in Engels's study of the conditions of the English working class.

If alienation means the substitution of humans' creative relationship to nature by a mere cash nexus, this endows money with extraordinary power that, according to Marx, it never enjoyed in precapitalist societies. In a powerful manuscript section called "On the Power of Money," Marx gives free rein to his classical literary education by quoting Goethe's *Faust* as well as Shakespeare's *Timon of Athens* to bring out the nature of money not just as a means of exchange but as a corporeal expression of its ability to endow its possessor with qualities he does not have as a person himself. He may be lame, but by being able to buy horses and carriages he becomes swift; he may be ugly, but money can buy him the most beautiful woman—so he is not ugly. Money transforms everything into its opposite.

> Money as the external universal medium and faculty . . . [turns] an image into reality and reality into mere image, transforms the real essential powers of man and nature into what are merely abstract notions.

All this presents Marx with a serious intellectual challenge: having castigated capitalist industrial society as basically dehumanizing, he has to suggest an alternative, and he does this in a manuscript called "Private Property and Communism." It is one of the very few instances where Marx tries to describe an alternative society—communism—transcending private property. As we shall also see later, Marx is careful not to fall into the pitfall of what he calls "utopian socialism"—concocting out of thin air a perfect alternative to capitalism. It would therefore not come as a surprise that in this case, when he does try to pick up the challenge, his descriptions of communist alternatives are at the same time accompanied by sharp criticisms of such attempts by other socialist thinkers.

VISIONS OF COMMUNISM

As Marx mentioned in the preface to *EPM*, the Paris years acquainted him with the writings of French—but also English —socialists, and the manuscript on "Private Property and Communism" clearly shows this. This section of the *EPM* reflects both Marx's brilliant powers of analysis as well as his formidable rhetorical flair—but also some of his limitations. It is inspiring, sometimes hauntingly beautiful—yet also somewhat disappointing. It also presents the reader with some methodological challenges that cannot always be resolved, given the fact that this is merely a rough manuscript, not a finally polished and edited text.

What stands out immediately in this manuscript is that Marx does not suggest a straightforward vision of communism, but speaks of different ways of abolishing private property, and different types of communism. What is not clear, however, is whether what he is describing are different *theories* of communism—some of which he finds inadequate—or whether these are various *stages* of communist developments in the future. The text is open to both interpretations, though on internal evidence of some of Marx's later writings, it seems that he is describing future historical stages of the development of communist societies. Be this as it may, what stands out in either interpretation is that for Marx there are inadequate forms of communism, which have to be transcended, and that communism to him does not mean just the mere nationalization of the means of production or a mechanical egalitarianism.

The first form of communism described by Marx is called "crude" or "raw" communism, and its major feature is the abolition of private property through nationalization. Yet to him this does not change the basic relationship between workers, their work, and the product of their labor—hence alienation is not yet overcome. This is merely "the generalization of private property. . . . The role of the worker is not abolished, but is extended to all men. The relationship of private property remains the relationship to the world of things."

The point made here by Marx is significant because so many socialist or communist visions or regimes viewed nationalization as the ultimate realization of their goals. In a number of long—and passionate—passages Marx takes issue with this position, and in the course of his criticism of this "crude communism" he gives expression to some of the more poetically moral foundations of his thought. The limits of this "crude communism" are evident to Marx:

> The domination of material property looms so large that it aims to destroy everything which cannot be possessed by everyone as private property. It wishes to eliminate talent, etc. by force. Immediate physical possession seems to be the unique goal of life and existence.

And then comes an extraordinary passage, in which Marx refers to the tendency of this form of communism to see in the breakup of the bourgeois family and the introduction of "free love" the ultimate victory over private property. To Marx, the opposite is true.

> This tendency to oppose general private property [that is, nationalization] to private property is expressed in an animal form: marriage . . . is contrasted with the community of women, in which women become communal and common property. . . . This is the open secret of this entirely crude and unreflective communism. Just as women are to pass from marriage to universal prostitution, so the whole world of wealth (i.e. the objective being of men) is to pass from the relation of exclusive marriage with the private owner to the relation of universal prostitution with the community. This communism negates the personality of man . . .
>
> This approach to women as the spoil and handmaid of communal lust is the expression of infinite degradation . . .
>
> The community is only a community of labor and equality of wages paid out by the communal capital—by the community as the universal capitalist. Both sides of the relationship are raised to an imagined universality . . .
>
> This is an abstract negation of the whole world of culture and civilization and the regression to the unnatural simplicity of the poor individual who has no needs and who has

not only not transcended private property but has not yet even attained it.

This is truly strong language: calling the nationalization of private property, the hallmark of many socialist ideologies, "prostitution with the community" is certainly rhetorical excess, but it shows how Marx's vision of a future socialist society was different—and deeper and more complex—from that of many of his radical colleagues. It clearly shows the weight of cultural baggage he brings to his vision of future society.

Yet before Marx moves to what he considers a higher form of communism, he adds a passionate—and revealing—passage about the nature of sexual relations, which he elevates to the quintessence of the meaning of humanity. It is a rare outburst, caused by Marx's lack of sympathy for ideas of "free love" that were current, especially among French radicals of the day and their supporters among the German exiles in Paris. Nowhere in his opus can one find a similar view of the relationship of man to woman as emblematic of men's (and women's) nature as a species. The language borders on the poetic, but again does not lose its analytical power. It may appear as if this outburst comes out of nowhere, but the terms Marx uses very carefully have their roots in his philosophical anthropology.

> The direct, natural and necessary relation of person to person is the relation of man [*Mann*] to woman. In this natural species-relationship the relation of man [*Mensch*] to nature is immediately his relation to man, just as his relation to man is immediately his relation to nature—to his own natural determination. Consequently, in this relationship it is sensuously manifested, reduced to an observable fact, the extent to which the human essence has become nature to man, or to which extent nature has become the human nature. From this relationship one can therefore judge man's whole level of development . . . how man as a species-being has come to be himself and to comprehend himself. The relation of man to

woman is the most natural relation of human being to human being, it therefore reveals the extent to which man's natural behavior has become human and his human behavior has become natural. [It] also reveals the extent to which man's need has become a *human* need—the extent to which *the other person as a person has become for him a need—the extent to which he in his individual existence is at the same time a social being* [italics added].

The obviously repetitive language is not only a reflection of the fact that this is a draft—but also that there is a passion here, rooted perhaps not only in philosophical insights but also in deeper personal layers of consciousness—something usually quite rare in Marx's ways of expressing himself.

After this extraordinary excursus, Marx returns to his discussion of various forms of communism: having expressed his devastating critique of what he calls "crude communism" and its destruction of culture, he briefly mentions other forms of communism that still maintain the existence of the state ("be it democratic or despotic"), which he therefore views as incomplete. It is only with the abolition (*Aufhebung*) of the state as such that Marx sees communism achieving its true aim—the abolition of human alienation.

The *Aufhebung* of the state, which appears again in Marx's later writings, has to be understood in the dialectical context of Hegelian philosophy. As already noted, *Aufhebung* covers, both in common German parlance as well as in the Hegelian system, a complex set of meanings: keeping, raising to a higher level—and abolition. In the specific case of the *Aufhebung* of the state one should bear in mind that what Marx means is that this ultimate form of communism both keeps the universal function attributed to the state, raises it to a higher level—and abolishes it as a separate and discrete institution. The Hegelian postulate of the state as the realm of the universal, communitarian nature of human relations is seen by Marx as being realized at the higher form of communism through the disappearance of the state as a separate institution, and hence the gap between civil society and the state—one of the institutional expressions of modern alienation—is overcome.

The problem, of course, is that Marx does not spell out what exactly is meant by this form of communism that he sees as the final goal of history. He endows this form of communism ("the positive transcendence of private property") with the highest possible attributes: "It is the definite resolution of the antagonism between man and nature and between man and man." He crowns this with the ultimate resolution of all the tensions of human history:

> It is the return of man to himself as a social, i.e. human, being, a return accomplished consciously and embracing the entire richness of previous development. This communism as fully developed naturalism equals humanism and as fully developed humanism equals naturalism.
>
> It is the true solution of the conflict between existence and essence,
>> between objectification and self-affirmation,
>> between freedom and necessity,
>> between the individual and the species.
>
> It is the solution of the riddle of history—and knows itself to be this solution.

Looking carefully at this messianic vision one soon realizes that the tensions to be overcome by this form of communism are actually the major tensions that traditional philosophy tried to solve. The terms used by Marx hark back to the challenges of Hegelian philosophy, from the *Phenomenology of the Spirit* to *The Philosophy of Right:* "Begriff/Wesen" (concept/essence, or being), "Existenz/Wesen" (existence/essence), "Vergegenständlichung/Selbstbestätigung" (objectification/self-assertion). Marx's highest form of communism is the answer to the riddle that philosophy tried to solve in the realm of thought but Marx maintains can be solved only through historical praxis.

But this powerful and inspiring apotheosis is also disappointing. Although Marx describes in great detail and harshly criticizes the forms of communism he views as incomplete (whether they are different theories of communism or stages of future communist development), when it comes to what he calls "the solution of the riddle of history that knows itself to be the solution" (a most extraordinary philosophical claim), he remains in the realm of philosophical statements, never following this up with a discussion of what this would mean in real, historical life.

In his *Theses on Feuerbach*, written at about the same time, Marx concludes with an equally powerful statement (Thesis 11): "Philosophers have until now only interpreted the world in various ways; but the point is to change it." This should not be seen as a denigration of philosophy as a useless scholastic exercise: on the contrary. Its meaning is that until that time, philosophers had only interpreted the world, but now, as Marx claims for his own philosophy, there exists an adequate interpretation of the world, and it is finally possible to change it. Changing the world is not the opposite of philosophy—it depends on philosophy's adequate interpretation of the world. This is what Marx was trying to do in his writings for the rest of his life, and therefore his unfinished major opus was titled *Das Kapital*—not *Der Sozialismus*. When Marx wrote the stirring passage about what the final form of communism would mean, he may have been aware that he could not go beyond these generalities, beautiful though disappointing as they may be. For him the quest for a historically adequate interpretation of the world is still the only key for changing it.

AGAINST ONE-DIMENSIONAL MATERIALISM

During the Brussels years, Marx tried to formulate systematically his thinking about Feuerbach's philosophy. This he did mainly in two very disparate pieces of writings—the short and pithy *Theses on Feuerbach* and the extensive *The German Ideology*, neither published in his lifetime, but critical to the construction of the dialectical nature of his materialist view of history.

Like all Young or Left Hegelians, Marx's indebtedness to Feuerbach was enormous, and is evident in his critique of Hegel in the *DFJ*. Feuerbach's *The Essence of Christianity* (1841) had a liberating impact on German philosophical and theological discourse in presenting what was called the "anthropological essence of religion." This led to a basically atheistic position claiming that religious thought is a human artifact projecting unto the deity the attributes human beings lack in their real life in the here and now. In this Feuerbach followed the legacy of eighteenth-century French materialist thought.

For Marx this was a powerful theoretical weapon in his critique of Hegel's idealist philosophy. Yet Marx found Feuerbach's thinking abstract, divorced from the real conditions of human life: the fact that various religions differ from one another has to do with different real-life social conditions. Therefore any attempt to overcome human alienation—which is reflected in religious thoughts and beliefs—has to study human social conditions, not religion itself.

Marx had already followed this line in his *DFJ* essays, but writing in Brussels he went one step further. Materialists, he argues, look at human perception of reality as if it were a merely automatic, passive activity—as if reality existed as such outside human consciousness, and human perception was merely registering it in a mechanical way. But—to Marx—the way human beings perceive objective reality is influenced and determined by the social conditions that have formed their consciousness: so human perception is not just a mechanical reflection of a reality "out there," but is mediated through the specific conditions that had formed the human beings who perceive it. In other words, Feuerbach's materialism overlooks the subjective ingredient in all human consciousness—be it that of individuals or of large human groups.

> The chief defect of all previous materialism (including Feuerbach's) is that the object, what we perceive through our senses, is understood only in the form of object or contemplation, but not as a sensuous human activity, as praxis, not subjectively. Hence in opposition to materialism the active side was developed abstractly by idealism.

Beyond the apparent scholarly language, this is a battle cry against the one-dimensionality of classical materialism, as represented by Feuerbach, which totally overlooks human agency and its role in the way human beings perceive reality. Hence the need to integrate the contribution of idealist philosophy (of Hegel) into a praxis-oriented way of thinking.

> The materialist doctrine of changing circumstances and education forgets that circumstances are changed by men and that the educator himself must be educated.

To Marx this also means that human agency can never be just individual, as human beings are *Gattungswesen* (species-being) and depend on interpersonal active relations. Religious contemplation is not sufficient to extricate human beings from their alienation either. By overlooking the role of human consciousness in the perception of reality, Feuerbach's passive materialism is ultimately conservative.

> The highest point attained by contemplative materialism . . . which does not comprehend sensuousness as practical activity, is the contemplation of separate individuals and of civil society [*bürgerliche Gesellschaft*]. . . . The standpoint of the new materialism is human society or social humanity.

Marx also argues that Feuerbach reduces individuals to their mere economic activities, and hence human practice "is understood and established only in its coarse Jewish manifestation and does not comprehend the significance of 'revolutionary,' of 'practical-critical' activity." As in the case of Bauer, Marx seems to recognize in Feuerbach's thinking echoes of pejorative Christian anti-Judaic images.

Marx's new materialism is presented as a dialectical synthesis of a philosophy anchored in traditional materialism but drawing at the same time on the subjective dimensions of human consciousness and agency implied in the idealist heritage: human beings start with a material objective reality, but man as *Homo faber* has the capacity of changing it through praxis. Human beings are products of nature, but their natural capacities give them the ability to change and transcend these conditions. Marx does not give this "new materialism" a name, and even in his later writings avoids the term, but this is the meaning of "dialectical materialism," which starts with nature but is not its prisoner. Hence the potential of what Marx refers to in the *Theses* as "revolutionary praxis."

The manuscript of *The German Ideology* is to a large extent carrying out the agenda implied in the *Theses*—to move from a philosophical discourse to looking at concrete, historical conditions in which people live and how they form their perceptions of reality and social praxis. Like *The Holy Family*, this is also a collection of disparate essays, many of them harsh and biting polemics; not surprisingly, Part 1 is called "Feuerbach." It is here that Marx presents for the first time and develops his theory of history, arguing that different forms of production give rise to different forms of social organization and political control.

> History is nothing but the succession of different generations, each of which exploits the material forces, the forms of capital, the productive forces handed down to it by all preceding ones and thus on the one hand continuing the traditional activity . . . and on the other hand modifies the old circumstances with completely new activities.

This historicity, which according to Marx is totally alien to Feuerbach's mechanistic materialism, is responsible for the emergence of political and legal institutions and norms that correspond to the underlying economic and social conditions. Forms of property are formulated accordingly, and consequently the dominant ideas of every society are nothing else than the ideas of its ruling groups and classes.

What follows in Marx's analysis is a theory of history related to modes of production, and each historical period is characterized by the specific ways human beings supply their needs—and create, in the process, new needs. Tribal or feudal property forms derive not from theoretical assumptions about the nature of "property as such," but from the interests of those who control the means of production. Where philosophers and economic theorists are misled, and mislead their readers and students, is in presenting these historically anchored arrangements of law and state as if they were eternal verities rather than expressions of conditions arising from specific historical circumstances and subject to further historical changes.

But therein lies a paradox: these historically anchored ideas—"ideologies," as Marx terms them—eventually attain an independent power over people's imagination and over time people tend to forget that they were human artifacts, brought up by their own consciousness, and thus humans become enslaved to them even when changing circumstances make them dysfunctional and irrelevant. This kind of "false consciousness" becomes a barrier to people's understanding of reality, and these gaps between actual reality and the way it is perceived by a given society create the tensions that bring about revolutions and historical change. One of the tasks of critical philosophy, Marx argues, is to reveal these ideologies for what they are and to tear away the veil they provide for the ruling classes. He follows this up with a social history of the way changing modes of production gave rise to different classes and ideas of law and property—from primitive common property through slave society, feudalism, and the modern, machine-driven industrial capitalist society.

These detailed historical studies in *The German Ideology* became the foundation of Marx's condensed account of world history in *The Communist Manifesto:* in a way, the *Manifesto* is the tip of a much deeper iceberg that Marx had detailed in *The German Ideology.* This is where he formulated his verdict that "the state is the form in which members of the ruling class realize their common interests and through which all institutions of its civil society are expressed."

As in his other writings, Marx does not discuss in detail the institutional structures of a future communist society, though he claims that "it differs from all previous movements in that it overturns all earlier relations of production." One of the premises of industrial production is the division of labor, which according to Marx just adds to human alienation, as it defines every person exclusively through his function in a chain of productive processes that he does not control. In a playful passage he contrasts this with how a future communist society would look:

> As soon as the division of labor is introduced, each man has a particular, exclusive sphere of activity, which is forced upon him and which he cannot escape. He is a hunter, a fisherman, a shepherd, or a critical critic . . .
>
> In communist society, where nobody has one exclusive sphere of activity but each can become accomplished in any branch he wishes, society regulates the general production and thus makes it possible for me to do one thing today and another tomorrow, to hunt in the morning, to fish in the afternoon, rear cattle in the evening and criticize after dinner, just as I have in mind, without ever becoming a hunter, fisherman, shepherd or critical critic.

This is indeed splendid, yet the bucolic examples (drawn from a draft by Fourier which Marx obviously makes fun of) of course do not give an adequate answer to what a post-division-of-labor industrial society would look like. In Fourier's plan, each person is allotted set hours every day for each of these activities (which actually preserve a coercive system, though a different one), but Marx's flight of imagination does at least focus on the emancipatory and liberating aspects of overcoming the division of labor, though it fails in terms of a concrete, workable proposal. By focusing on pre-industrial occupations, he avoids the much trickier answer to the question of how the division of labor can be overcome in an industrial society. This did not prevent his edenic postulate from becoming immensely popular, especially among New Age socialists.

TOWARD *THE COMMUNIST MANIFESTO*

Marx's prolific writing activity in the Paris and Brussels years was embedded in the political activities of various radical groups that brought together émigré German artisans and intellectuals with French and later also English activists. As it often happens with radical groups, especially in exile, internal schisms and disagreements sometimes loomed larger than concrete activities, clandestine or public, against the powers that be. Despite their relative insignificance, these groups and their members were under the constant surveillance and scrutiny of the political police in different continental countries, leading, as we have seen, to Marx's expulsion from France and his move to Brussels.

What characterized these groups, despite their marginality, was that they brought together radicals from different countries and thus created a common European revolutionary ambience, though the disparate groups never coalesced into a coherently organized movement. Among the various groups, whose names constantly changed, one of the more significant ones was called the League of the Just (Bund der Gerechten), which started initially as a German conspiratorial gathering but then reached out to French and English radicals of various stripes—French followers of Auguste Blanqui, British Chartists and Christian socialists. The league's motto was "All Men are Brothers," clearly echoing Friedrich Schiller's "Ode to Joy" [Alle Menschen werden Brüder]. In one of these groups, which became known as the Communist Correspondence Society, Marx served for some time as coordinating secretary. After numerous internal debates and quarrels, at a meeting in London in June 1847—which Marx could not attend—it changed its name to the League of Communists (Bund der Kommunisten), absorbing the Brussels-based Correspondence Society. At another meeting, in November 1847, also in London (which Marx did attend), a decision was made to publish a founding manifesto, and Marx and Engels were asked prepare it.

Marx finished the final German draft in January 1848. Because of censorship laws on the Continent, it was printed in February 1848 in London under the auspices of the innocuously named "Workers Educational Association," with an address in the East End (46 Liverpool Street, Bishopgate). The pamphlet does not mention the names of either Marx or Engels as authors. Translations into English, French, Italian, Danish, and Flemish were promised in the prefatory note, but only Polish and Danish translations followed; an English translation appeared for the first time only in 1850 in a serialized form in a Chartist paper.

A few days after the *Manifesto*'s initial publication, the February Revolution broke out in Paris—unexpected by the authors of the pamphlet as by everyone else—triggering the revolutions of 1848–49 across Europe. The *Manifesto* was hardly noticed, and Marx's name was not connected to it publicly. The League of Communists did not play any significant role in any of the 1848 revolutions, even though in the later Marxist narrative, the two became almost inseparable.

Yet the *Manifesto*'s obscurity on publication stands in stark contrast to its eventual theoretical and historical significance: despite its relative brevity, it certainly is one of the most significant statements of Marx's thought, and its posthumous fame, especially after the Soviet Revolution, gave it a world-historical resonance. Even if the role ascribed to it by the Communist parties of the twentieth century is wholly unmerited and historically false, its combination of a profound historical analysis with powerful rhetoric justifies placing it as a defining text in the pantheon of world history. Comparison to the Sermon on the Mount may not be an exaggeration.

5

The Communist Manifesto *and*
the Revolutions of 1848

OF ALL OF MARX'S WRITINGS, *The Communist Manifesto* is undoubtedly the one best known and clearly most influential. It is a bravura performance, with lapidary slogans that have echoed across generations and continents: "All history is the history of class struggle"; "The workers have no homeland"; "The proletariat has nothing to lose but its chains"; "Workers of all countries—unite." Millions of people—from academics to workers and peasants—immediately recognize them.

Yet much of this is also misleading, including the very title of the work. Written, as we have seen, for a group of radicals who called themselves the League of Communists, it was published as *The Manifesto of the Communist Party*—which sounded, especially after the Russian Revolution of 1917, as if it were the forerunner of the Bolshevik wing of the Russian Social Democratic Workers Party that renamed itself after seizing power as the Russian (and later Soviet) Communist Party. The document from 1848 thus appeared as its legitimate progenitor.

But the League of Communists, of course, was nothing like a modern organized political party. Marx used the term "Party" (*Partei*) in a much less rigid and more fluid sense—as we have seen in Engels's report on socialist activity in Germany: it meant "group" or "tendency," especially in a period when the existence of modern political parties was still rather embryonic. But there is no doubt that attaching the term "Party" to what was basically a loose group of corresponding societies, without a distinct organization structure, gave the *Manifesto* an image of power and possible influence it did not possess at the time of its publication. When republished with a new introduction by Marx and Engels in 1873, in a totally different political environment, it endowed the 1848 text with a posthumous aura that it continued to possess in the following decades. And as we shall see later, it had very little impact on the dramatic developments of the European revolutions of 1848–49, and it did not foresee their outbreak a few weeks after its publication.

HISTORICAL ANALYSIS AND REVOLUTIONARY PROGRAM

The text of the *Manifesto* itself moves, sometimes uneasily, between two levels of discourse: on one hand, the soaring world-historical analysis of the relationship between social classes and political power, and comments, somewhat marginally and certainly ephemerally about the attitude of the League of Communists to various radical social groups in France, Germany, and England, coupled with a searing critique of other socialist groups. In both cases the *Manifesto* expresses in pithy and concise language the fruits of Marx's studies in the previous years, when he formed his own theories about historical development as well as his critique of practically every other socialist thinker or school. Writing the *Manifesto* forced Marx to distill complex arguments into catchy phrases: this is the work's great achievement, but it sometimes presents Marx's complex arguments in what may appear as simplistic catchwords if one is not aware of the enormous preparatory work that went into them.

The opening paragraph of the *Manifesto* has become the doctrinal foundation of latter-day Marxism. Marx's own post-1848 studies have presented a much more nuanced and differentiated analysis of class and politics, both in France and in Germany; but the resounding cadences of the powerful opening paragraph have been presented, both by followers of Marx as well as by his opponents and critics, as if they are the quintessential sum of his social philosophy:

> The history of all hitherto existing society is the history of class struggle. Freeman and slave, patrician and plebeian, lord and serf, guild-master and journeyman—in a word, oppressor and oppressed, stood in constant opposition to one another, carried an uninterrupted, sometimes hidden, sometimes open fight that each time ended either in a revolutionary reconstitution of society at large, or in the common ruin of the contending classes.

Marx then moves to describe the social and economic conditions brought about by the rise of bourgeois society: polarization between bourgeois and proletarians, the increasing pauperization and alienation of the working class leading to rising social tensions. The more capitalism develops, "the bourgeoisie produces, above all, its own grave-diggers. Its fall and the victory of the proletariat are equally inevitable." The social studies Marx undertook in the *EPM* and *The German Ideology* in great detail are now spelled out in the staccato phrases of the *Manifesto*.

Yet the most intriguing passage in Marx's description of the rise and working of bourgeois society is his extensive and detailed analysis of the role of the industrial revolution in demystifying the world and reducing all human relations to a mere cash nexus.

> Historically, the bourgeoisie has played a most revolutionary role. The bourgeoisie, wherever it has got the upper hand, has put an end to all feudal, patriarchal, idyllic relations. It has pitilessly torn asunder the motley feudal ties that bound man to his "natural superior," and has left remaining no other nexus between man and man than the naked self-interest, the callous "cash payment." . . . It has resolved personal worth into exchange value, and in place of the indefeasible chartered freedoms has set up the single unconscionable freedom —Free Trade. . . . The bourgeoisie has torn away from the family its sentimental veil, and has reduced the family relation to a mere money relation.

The inner logic of the capitalist mode of production necessarily leads to a novel phenomenon—for the first time in history creating a world market, based on the necessity for constant change.

> The bourgeoisie cannot exist without constantly revolutionizing the instruments of production and thereby the relations of production and with them the whole relations of society. . . . The need for a constant expanding market for its products chases the bourgeoisie over the whole surface of the globe. It must nestle everywhere, settle everywhere, establish connections everywhere. The bourgeoisie has through its expansion of the world market given a cosmopolitan character to production and consumption in every country . . .
>
> In place of the old needs, satisfied by the products of the country, we find new needs, requiring for their satisfaction the products of distant lands and climes. . . . The bourgeoisie draws even the most barbaric nations into civilization. The cheap prices of the commodities are the heavy artillery with which it batters down all Chinese walls, with which it forces the barbarians' intensely obstinate hatred of foreign-

ers to capitulate. It forces all nations, on the pain of extinction, to adopt the bourgeois mode of production.

By creating a world economy, this globalization of material production and the creation of new, globally anchored needs has profound impacts on all spheres of life, beyond the mere material. The philosophical and rich literary background of Marx's schooling and research becomes clearly evident in a passage showing that his economic studies have not left him unaware of the spiritual dimension of human existence and historical development.

> In place of the old local and national seclusion and self-sufficiency we have universal interdependence of nations.
> And as in material, so also in intellectual production. The intellectual creations of individual nations become common property. National one-sidedness and narrow-mindedness become more and more impossible, and from the numerous national and local literatures there arises a world literature.

Marx's radical critique of capitalist society did not prevent him from overlooking its enormous revolutionary role in bringing about what would be called today globalization, which creates not only a world market but also a world culture.

THE TEN REGULATIONS: A PROGRAM FOR
REVOLUTIONARY TRANSFORMATION

This ode to the bourgeoisie is of course dialectically subversive: it is precisely the revolutionary nature of capitalism in overhauling all hitherto existing conditions and its universal expansion that create the conditions for its internal *Aufhebung* and its replacement by the proletariat. More than in any of his writings, on this occasion Marx provided the most detailed program for this transformation: it is the closest he ever came to providing a plan for the proletarian revolution's transformation of capitalism into a socialist society. Yet its sophistication, hidden behind its trenchant language, has sometimes escaped the attention of both Marx's followers and his critics.

The program a revolutionary government should enact, according to Marx, consists of a list of ten specific measures, although these are prefaced with his customary caution: the measures, he writes, "will of course be different in different countries." He underlines the fact that the revolutionary transformation will not be a one-time act that would change things overnight: he maintains that the proletariat "will wrest, *by degrees*, all capital from the bourgeoisie," and further admits that initially this will be undertaken "by measures which appear economically insufficient and untenable."

Yet this careful language should not mislead. Marx states explicitly that even these apparently limited measures have to be "effected by means of despotic inroads on the rights of property and on the conditions of bourgeois production." The apparent tension between the initially careful language and the subsequent reference to despotic means becomes clear only by carefully parsing what follows: the Ten Regulations that he suggests will need to be enacted. Marx proposes that these would apply "pretty generally in the most advanced countries," even though they may vary from country to country. The list, revealing as it is, also hides some surprising omissions, and has to be read in toto in order to realize its complexity and cunning.

1. Abolition of property in land and the application of all rents of land to public purposes.
2. A heavy progressive or graduated income tax.
3. Abolition of all rights of inheritance.
4. Confiscation of the property of all emigrants and rebels.
5. Centralization of all credits in the hands of the state. . . .
6. Centralization of the means of communication and transport in the hands of the state.

7. Extension of factories and instruments of production owned by the state. . . .
8. Equal obligation of all to work. Establishment of industrial armies, especially for agriculture.
9. Combination of agriculture with manufacturing industry; gradual abolition of all the distinctions between town and country. . . .
10. Free education for all children in public schools. Abolition of children's factory labor in its present form. Combination of education with industrial production.

This is obviously a drastic program, justifying Marx's description of its measures as "despotic inroads into property rights." Yet despite what appears as sweeping nationalization, *it does not include the immediate abolition of private property rights of the owners of industry.* By contrast, it envisions a lengthy and gradual process, not a one-time act of expropriation and nationalization. This is the extremely sophisticated secret of this program: it is about a process, not a legislative fiat.

Let us go through the Ten Regulations one by one and see how nuanced and differentiated these measures are and how seriously Marx does not follow revolutionary slogans but tries to imagine how the machinery of the revolution should really work.

The Ten Regulations call for an extensive—but not total—abolition of private property rights. Private property in land is abolished (measure number 1), banks and the means of transportation (mainly railroads) are nationalized (measures 5 and 6)—but the owners of industry do not have their property immediately expropriated. They will be subject to a heavy progressive income tax (measure 2); it is only if they flee the country or are involved in rebellious activities that their property will be confiscated (measure 4); and they will not be able to leave their property to their descendants (measure 3). In the meantime, they may continue to own their factories, but will have to compete in the market against a public industrial sector set up by the state (measure 7). This public industrial sector, made up from industrial property expropriated from émigrés and rebels as well as from deceased owners whose property reverts to the state, will naturally enjoy preferential treatment from the state-owned bank and railways.

In other words: private industrial property, while not immediately nationalized, will be slowly, but surely, squeezed out of existence; its owners, unless they emigrate or rebel, will be able to continue to function, albeit under disadvantage—high taxes, competition with preferred state-owned industries. The abolition of private ownership of the means of industrial production will take place gradually and will certainly come to an end within one generation due to the abolition of the rights of inheritance.

By proposing this gradual and differentiated scheme Marx shows his understanding of the dynamics of industrial production—and of social psychology. While many radical socialists have called for immediate expropriation of all means of production, especially industrial ownership, Marx is aware that such a step would entail a major disruption of industrial production and thus confront the revolutionary government with a deep economic and financial crisis (which indeed has happened in those cases where such drastic steps have been taken). Moreover, this would also push the industrial bourgeoisie into a corner and transform many of its members into active opponents of the revolution: if they have nothing to lose, as their property has been confiscated anyway, and since they and their families were made into paupers, why should they not become active rebels and saboteurs? Marx, on the other hand, offers them the possibility of continuing to live more or less as they have been used to, implicitly also allowing them to place their children in the new social order.

Through the nuanced brutality of the complex structure

introduced by the Ten Regulations, the capitalist owners of industry become, nilly-willy, passive accomplices in the socialist revolution and in their own extinction as a class; but it does not force them into the counterrevolutionary camp. Marx may not have been aware of Machiavelli's advice to the Prince not to confiscate the property of enemies he executes: their children, he maintained in one of his more chilling statements, will more easily forgive the murder of their parents than the confiscation of their inheritance.

While the sophisticated measures dealing with transforming private into public property over time are the bedrock of the logic of the Ten Regulations, they also include other measures that are both quite despotic but deeply transformative. The imposition of a universal duty to be part of the working population and the creation of labor brigades involving overcoming the distinction between town and country (measures 8 and 9) are accompanied by what may look surprising: his guarded statement about the abolition of child labor "in its present form" (measure 10). Keeping in mind that Marx viewed labor—the transformation of nature and man's self-realization—as the foundation of every human being as *Homo faber*, one can well follow the logic of his thinking: free education for all children should not mean just classical humanistic education, but an attempt to prepare the young for a life of labor—obviously not under the horrible conditions of the industrial revolution. Making every child study philosophy and learn Latin and Greek (as Marx himself did) is not the answer: education should be universal, but attuned to each human's role as a creator.

Marx has no problem calling the Ten Regulations the expression of the dictatorship of the proletariat (one of the few instances he uses the term). Yet using the term in this specific context means both more and less than one imagines. To Marx, all political power is a dictatorship—the rule of one class over the other, so the proletarian revolution in its first, political stage as expressed by the Ten Regulations is no exception. If capital-ism is the dictatorship of the bourgeoisie, the despotic measures of the Ten Regulations are obviously the dictatorship of the proletariat.

The only difference—and what according to Marx grants the dictatorship of the proletariat legitimacy—is that this dictatorship is of the majority over the minority, while all previous forms of government were the dictatorship of a minority. Hence he adds what appears to be both a contradiction and a piece of cynical propaganda: "The first step in the revolution by the working class is to raise the proletariat to the position of ruling class, to win the battle of democracy." But to him it is obvious and in a way self-evident, given the meaning of democracy as majority rule.

Yet as in the *EPM*, Marx is aware that this first stage of communism—the rule of the proletariat as the dominant class—cannot be the ultimate goal of the revolution, nor is it yet the true realization of socialism. He therefore goes on to suggest that the Ten Regulations are merely a necessary step toward the transcendence—*Aufhebung*—of political power as such. But just as in the *EPM*, his language, while inspiring, remains vague.

> When in the course of development, class distinctions have disappeared, and all production has been concentrated in the hands of a vast association of the whole nation, the public power will lose its political character. . . . The working class will then have abolished its own supremacy as a class.

Again, Marx is true to his own principles of not being able or willing to give a full picture of a distant future. So before moving on to the critique of utopian socialism, he ends this section of the *Manifesto* with a soaring passage that certainly can also be criticized as utopian—though the Ten Regulations suggest that when it comes to the proximate and immediate steps of the future revolution, Marx was at least far more con-crete than those he was criticizing:

In place of the old bourgeois society, with its classes and class antagonisms, we shall have an association in which the free development of each is the condition for the free development of all.

Looking at this in the context of Marx's previous writings, one sees a clear reference here to the social essence of the human as *Homo faber*, where labor brings out both individual self-realization as well as the immanent need for the other.

The following sections of the *Manifesto* deal with various socialist thinkers and movements and then with how the League of Communists relates to different radical, not necessarily socialist, groups in various European countries. This section is of less theoretical interest and in many respects repeats what he wrote previously on these issues. There is, however, a somewhat surprising comment about Germany.

One would expect Marx to assume that the revolution would first break out in the most industrially developed country— England. Yet in a strategically insightful passage he expresses a totally different view.

It is to Germany that the Communists chiefly turn their attention, because that country is on the eve of a bourgeois revolution that is bound to be carried out under more advanced conditions of European civilization and with a much more developed proletariat than that of England was in the 17th century and that of France in the 18th century, and because the bourgeois revolution in Germany will be but the prelude to an immediately following proletarian revolution.

It may of course also be that this identification of Germany as the focus of the next revolution had to do with the fact that the League of Communists, for all its internationalist aims and ideology, was primarily an association of German revolutionaries. Nevertheless, this pivot to the least developed major European society as the weak link of the existing order suggests a dialectical rather than a mere linear grasp of historical development. It would also determine to a large extent the trajectory of Marx's activities during the revolutionary years of 1848–49. Germany, rather than England or France, would be the center of his theoretical and practical efforts. It was of course also his own country.

1848 AND THE *NEUE RHEINISCHE ZEITUNG*

Like everyone else, Marx was taken by surprise by the outbreak of the 1848 revolutions—which started in late February in Paris, quickly followed by uprisings in mid-March in Vienna, Budapest, and Berlin, and in most western continental European capitals. The post-1815 conservative Restoration, with its reactionary and oppressive politics, appeared to have come to an end. Monarchy was abolished in France, most crowned heads yielded to demands for elections, provisional governments were established, elected parliaments were rapidly convened. Perhaps the most notable of these changes was the convening in Frankfurt in May 1848 of the first elected all-German National Assembly. It appeared that representative governments were about to be set up, and in Germany and Italy national unification seemed all of a sudden a distinct possibility, combining liberalism and nationalism.

The Democratic Association in Brussels, of which Marx was one of its leading members, immediately sent a congratulatory letter to the Provisional Government in Paris, which responded by rescinding the 1845 order that had expelled Marx and some of his colleagues from France. At the same time, the Belgian government, which tried to keep above the fray, expelled Marx from Brussels, and on 4th March, he and his family left for Paris.

During the following months, Marx was involved in two parallel tracks. He continued his activity in the League of Communists, the center of which had moved to Paris; it maintained that what was happening was an all-European eruption and was looking forward to pushing the revolutionary energy toward socialist goals. At the same time, it is obvious that Marx focused primarily on developments in Germany, where the major issue was promoting—along with moderate liberals—German unification.

The tension between these two agendas becomes clear in a document written by Marx but also signed by Engels, Wilhelm Wolff (one of Marx's closest friends in the League of Communists), and others, on behalf of the League and published in Paris in late March, subsequently republished in German radical newspapers once censorship had been lifted.

The document starts with the battle cry of *The Communist Manifesto* ("Proletarians of all countries, unite!")—but its first paragraph deals with Germany and demands that "The whole of Germany shall be declared a single indivisible republic." It goes on to call for an elected all-German national assembly, defines who shall be eligible to vote, and calls for the abolition of all feudal and seigniorial rights—implying the dismantling of the various royal and ducal powers of the thirty-seven different German states as established by the Congress of Vienna. In combining this call for German unification with demanding that "the estates of princes and other feudal estates and all mines, pits etc. shall become the property of the state," it echoes, though in a slightly attenuated way, regulation number 1 of the *Manifesto*.

Echoes of the *Manifesto*'s socialist ideas, albeit in a milder form, can be further gleaned from the document: a state bank should replace private banking and be the sole source of credit; railways should be nationalized; "severely progressive" taxation should be introduced and consumption taxes abolished; there should be "restrictions on the right of inheritance" (not its total abolition as suggested in the *Manifesto*); universal popular education should be introduced, and national workshops established. To all this a "complete separation of church and state" is also added.

This is obviously a wish list much more than a program, and it is not at all clear what institutions should be set up to carry out these actions. Clearly the document was written under the immediate impact of the surprising developments of the first weeks of the revolutions that swept both France and Germany. The oscillation between a German nationalist agenda and calls for radical socialist measures shows that, although in the *Manifesto* Marx envisaged the proposed Ten Regulations as a program for a proletarian revolution, here he and his colleagues were not altogether clear whether they were at a threshold of democratic republicanism, German national unification—or the beginning of a radical all-European socialist revolution.

But what became clear on a personal level was Marx's decision to return to Germany. In 1845 he had renounced his Prussian citizenship so as not to fall even indirectly under the jurisdiction of his country of birth. Now he and his colleagues were able to renew their contacts with the people in Cologne who in 1842–43 had helped to set up the *Rheinische Zeitung*, and on 12th April 1848, Marx arrived in Cologne to take up the position of editor-in-chief of the newly established *Neue Rheinische Zeitung*. He was accompanied by Engels, who left his family business in Manchester to join in the revolutionary developments. The paper's first issue appeared on 31st May 1848; Marx held the position of editor until the *NRZ* was closed by the authorities a year later.

This was a year of turbulent activities for Marx, as the editor for a paper that called itself the "Organ for Democracy" and was not identified with the much more radical ideas of the League of Communists, of which he continued to be a member. As editor, Marx advocated mainly democratic and constitutional reforms and supported the liberal attempts, centered on the National Assembly in Frankfurt, to set up a unified German state, even if the only way of reaching this outcome would fall far short of the initial goal of establishing a German democratic republic. At the same time, his leading articles in the *NRZ* supported the (failed) Paris workers insurrection in June 1848, and his own travels to Berlin and Vienna brought him in contact with radical groups close to the League of Communists.

Yet it is clear that the soaring language of the *Manifesto* was aiming at the ultimate goal of a proletarian revolution growing out of the internal contradictions of the capitalist mode of production. The sudden and unexpected revolutions of 1848, on the other hand, were not going to lead directly to this historical denouement. Hence most of Marx's writings in the *NRZ* addressed issues connected with internal German topics: following the debates in the National Assembly in Frankfurt, attacking various German authorities in matters of civil rights and freedom of the press, as the *NRZ* itself was occasionally closed periodically, accused of inciting violence. But basically Marx disagreed with some of the more radical members of the League of Communists who would have liked to boycott elections and call for active revolutionary confrontation with the authorities. At the same time, in April 1849 the *NRZ* published a series of theoretical articles by Marx, titled "Wage Labor and Capital," with a socialist message that was unmistakable.

In the autumn of 1848 the authorities in most European countries succeeded in overcoming their initial shock and regained some control over the situation. In Vienna, Berlin, and Budapest, as well as in some of the Italian states, the revolutionary wave appeared to have run its course. Some of the bourgeois liberal groups, which initially supported the call for representative and constitutional government, now became frightened and coalesced with conservative forces against the more radical democratic demands, and in a series of articles Marx was among the first to identify these reversals. Because of Russia's intervention in support of the governments in the Habsburg lands, Marx even supported views calling for a war against Russia—one of the first intimations of his later concern about the role a

reactionary Russia might play in undermining democratic movements in Europe in the future.

The movement toward German unification eventually came
to an end when King Friedrich Wilhelm IV of Prussia declined
the National Assembly's offer of the title of German emperor.
The imperial crown, the king maintained, could not be granted
by an elected assembly, and the Frankfurt Assembly never recovered from this refusal.

Marx's articles in the *NRZ* reflected his awareness that the
revolutionary waves were receding and that the powers-that-be
were able, with some adjustments, to regain control and reassert
themselves. He followed these developments closely, and as we
have seen he made the point that the revocation of the civil
rights granted to the Jews in the German states under the initial pressures of the revolutionary impact was indicative of the
growing strength of the reactionary forces.

Attempting to block the reassertion of reactionary powers,
armed insurrections broke out in some of the smaller German
states—including Dresden in Saxony, and later in the historically liberal southwestern state of Baden. Engels joined the
insurgents, but their defeat also signified the end of the *NRZ*,
which the Prussian authorities finally closed in May 1849; the
final issue, printed in red ink, was published on 19th May. The
issue included a fiery poem by Ferdinand Freiligrath, a close
colleague of Marx in the League of Communists, which called
on the workers not to lose hope—but also not to follow provo-
cations that may lead to a failed insurrection and bloody suppression by the reinvigorated authorities.

Subsequently, Marx and his colleagues left Cologne for
Frankfurt and Baden, eventually leaving Germany altogether.
Marx arrived in Paris in early June; a few weeks later the last
insurrection in Baden was crushed. In France, the rise of Louis-
Napoleon Bonaparte to the presidency and later to the impe-
rial title as Napoleon III made it obvious that Paris, which had

served as a relative safe haven for German, Italian, Polish, Russian, and other democrats and radicals under the bourgeois monarchy of Louis-Philippe in the 1830s and 1840s, would no longer be hospitable to their presence or ideas. In late August 1849, Marx departed with his family, for London, where he lived for the rest of his life.

The revolutionary period of 1848–49 was the only time in Marx's life when he directly participated in revolutionary activity—mostly as an editor, but also through his leadership roles in the League of Communists. At its height, the League had about five hundred members. It never was a significant player in the 1848 revolutions, although the *NRZ* was an important organ of democracy in Germany, mainly in the liberal Rhineland. Marx was never to return to live permanently in Germany, and he was never involved again in direct revolutionary activity.

6

---·◆·◆·◆---

London: From Abject Penury to Middle-Class Existence

WHEN MARX AND HIS FAMILY arrived in London, he was a penniless exile who joined an increasing number of European radicals finding asylum in Britain. While political reaction was triumphing on the Continent, Britain's relatively liberal politics—and the fact that it had not been itself convulsed by the 1848–49 upheavals—turned London into the only place in Europe where radical politics could continue, after a fashion, to be carried out.

British radical groups, and especially the Chartists, were trying to help these destitute exiles, but their growing number exhausted whatever limited assistance could be offered, and most of these expatriates faced years of poverty and misery.

This was also the fate of Marx and his family during their first years in London. Like the other exiles, Marx continued initially to be active in the various revolutionary groups that tried to reconstitute themselves on British soil. He also attempted to pursue his economic studies, while publishing a number of essays on the current political development on the Continent; but his early years in London were the most terrible time of his—and his family's—life.

These years were a constant struggle for sheer survival, which took its toll on the family. Marx at that time had no sources of income, and was able to scrape by only though the generosity of some of his better situated German exile colleagues, like the poet Freiligrath. Later on, Ferdinand Lassalle, who emerged as the leader of the new German working-class association—the first successful German socialist movement— helped Marx generously several times, as did Engels, who went back to Manchester and reestablished himself as manager of his family's business there. Marx had exhausted the initial funds from his inheritance, and attempts to draw bills on his mother's name only caused further friction with her. Marx and his family moved from one cramped dwelling to another, eventually settling from 1850 to 1855 in rooms at 28 Dean Street in Soho. From time to time the family had to pawn whatever family heirlooms Jenny had brought with her, and Marx barely avoided being thrown into debtor's prison.

More children were born, but not all survived. Two of them, Guido and Franziska, born in London, died at the age of one year each in 1850 and 1851. In 1855, Marx's oldest son, Edgar, died, and at the same time Jenny gave birth to a still-born child. When Jenny's health continued to fail, the family could not afford a doctor, and in one harrowing case Marx had to borrow money for the funeral of one of their children. On another extreme occasion he had to pawn his coat, and consequently could not leave home.

These terrible conditions and pressures also appear to have had their impact on relations between the Marx couple. The deep romantic attachment between the aristocratic Jenny von Westphalen and her husband has survived the vagaries of persecution, exile, and destitute poverty caused by his revolutionary commitment. It has often been commented upon as extraordinary, and Jenny's belief in her companion is indeed remarkable, documented in their correspondence, in their continuous mutual professions of love and companionship. This comes out also in Jenny's memoir, which was published many years after the couple's death, showing not only a deep mutual love but also their sharing common beliefs and political views. Jenny, well-read and highly educated, was an intellectual companion to her husband, which is what drew the two together in the first place. Yet a disturbing crisis occurred in 1851—perhaps the worst year in their early exile in London.

When the young couple left Germany for Paris in 1843, soon after their marriage, Jenny's mother sent along with them her maid, Helene ("Lenchen") Demuth, who stayed with them as housekeeper throughout their exile in Paris, Brussels, and London. Despite the extra financial burden of having to provide for an additional soul, this obviously made even their most difficult years somewhat easier—living with them, taking care of the household, the children, and Jenny's frequent confinements. On 23rd June 1851, in their one-and-a-half-room apartment in Soho, Lenchen gave birth to a son.

The circumstances surrounding the birth of this child out of wedlock, named Alfred ("Freddy") Demuth, were shrouded in mystery for a long time. After his birth the boy was given out for adoption to a working-class family in London's East End. His birth certificate does not mention a father, but Engels—who frequently visited London—claimed paternity, and given his bachelor status and knowledge of his relationships with working-class women in Manchester, this was accepted in the family circles. Freddy occasionally visited his birth mother at the various homes of the Marx family, and the Marx daughters knew him as Lenchen's son and played with him.

Only close to his death in 1895 did Engels confess that Freddy's father was in fact Marx, and the reason he had accepted paternity was to preserve the Marx marriage. Marx's daughters were stunned to learn that their occasional playmate was really their half-brother, and kept the information to themselves. The truth came out only in the 1960s from some documents discovered by biographers of Marx's daughter Eleanor. Occasionally this was contested by some Marxists, especially in the Soviet Union, but there is no serious doubt today about Marx's paternity.

At the time the secret was well kept, and left no trace in the Marx-Engels correspondence; neither can it be ascertained whether the relationship between Marx and the family maid (so typical in nineteenth-century bourgeois households) was a one-time occasion or a longer liaison. Obviously it signified a crisis in the family, but it appeared to have been overcome, and if it left scars, they are not visible in what can be gleaned from the family history in the following decades.

Lenchen stayed in the Marx household, and when both Karl and Jenny died, she moved to Engels's home and managed his household; literate and politically engaged herself, she also helped Engels arrange and organize Marx's papers and manuscripts. Following her death, in 1890, she was buried in the grave of Karl and Jenny Marx at Highgate Cemetery, and her name is inscribed on the family tombstone. Freddy eventually learned about his true paternity from his half-sister Eleanor, who shared some of her inheritance with him. He was trained as a toolmaker, joined the Labour Party, and died in 1929, never publicly divulging his secret.

All this was happening against the background of Marx's intense activity among the German and other European exiles in London. As sometimes happens in similar situations, many of these exiles viewed their sojourn abroad as a merely temporary setback, hoping that they would be able to go back to their countries and continue their activities, not always realizing that tectonic changes had been taking place that made such hopes irrelevant. It appears that this was also Marx's initial view, but unlike many others of his colleagues in the League of Communists, he was one of the first to realize gradually that the new situation on the Continent called for a reassessment of his earlier thinking.

Through colleagues in Hamburg—which, as a Hansa Free City, was allowed to maintain a more liberal press law—Marx was able to revive for some time the *NRZ* as a periodical renamed *NRZ Revue*, where he published some of his essays dealing with the 1848 revolutions and their aftermath. But most of his efforts, like those of his fellow exiles in London, were devoted to maintaining whatever remained of their earlier organizational structures. So in September 1849, barely two months after arriving in London, Marx and some of his colleagues reconstituted themselves as the new central committee of the League of Communists. A few months later, after Engels returned to England, having survived the failed radical insurrection in Baden, both prepared on its behalf a lengthy "Address of the Central Committee of the League of Communists." It was printed in London, and the attempt to smuggle copies into Germany basically failed, so it had a very limited impact at the time; yet it is indicative of the somewhat confused state of mind of Marx in these first months of his exile in London.

On one hand, the "Address" maintains that the *Communist Manifesto* had proved to be the only correct analysis of the political situation in Europe—a claim that could hardly be vindicated by what happened during the revolutions of 1848 as well as in their suppression. It then contradicts itself by accusing the liberal bourgeoisie of the "betrayal of the revolutionary movement"—which is exactly the opposite of what the *Manifesto* foresaw as the role of the bourgeoisie in a coming revolution. But after this, the text tries to explain why further developments would be more complicated, why the Communist League needed to adopt a more extended time perspective, and suggests tactical steps to be taken to maintain its drive. The "Address" calls for radical demands (such as nationalization of all factories, which the *Manifesto* avoided), yet ends up with a generalized exhortation to the workers "to do their utmost for their eventual victory."

The ambivalent and somewhat contradictory language of this text clearly suggested the dilemmas and tensions faced by the members of the League of Communists in London, and they came to the surface within a few months. A radical faction, led by some of its veteran members, like the former army officer August Willich, who advocated resumption of revolutionary and clandestine activities, viewed the defeat of the revolution in 1849 as a mere temporary setback. In the ensuing internal debates, Marx called Willich and his supporters "alchemists of revolution," and toward the end of 1850 the League split, as did its London-based German Workers' Educational Association. Its headquarters were moved to Cologne, which effectively limited its ability to act and eventually led to its penetration by Prussian secret agents and the arrest of its local members and their trial. In November 1852, Marx moved to dissolve the rump League, claiming that the move to Cologne and the trial there of its activists had in fact put an end to its existence and its raison d'être. Willich eventually emigrated, like many German Forty-Eighters, to America, and distinguished himself as a brigadier general in the Union Army during the Civil War.

These internal splits—acrimonious and sometimes petty, as such developments usually are among exile groups—did reflect, however, a fundamental reassessment of Marx's own thinking, which he expressed in his writings during those years. While these writings never explicitly criticized his own statement in the *Manifesto*, they clearly suggested a significant revision. They also accentuate the difference between texts like the *Manifesto*, the aim of which was mainly ideological and propagandistic on behalf of a radical, revolutionary organization, and Marx's own analytical pieces, where he was speaking for himself.

Toward the mid-1850s Marx's personal financial situation slowly changed. With diminishing hopes for a reawakened revolutionary activity—and the dismantling of the League of Communists—Marx was able to establish himself as a contributor to various democratic journals on the Continent (*Die Presse* in Vienna, the *Neue Oder Zeitung* in Germany) as well as among the German émigré press in the United States. Some improvements in his personal fortunes also came his way, and the Marx family was able to extricate itself from the terrible conditions of their first years in London. Financial difficulties never left Marx, but at this time they were on another level: it was not a question of survival anymore, but of maintaining a decent, middle-class existence in a comfortable house in Hampstead, and trying to give his daughters a respectable education. His perennial financial struggles did not end, but at least the terrible years of poverty were over. Marx slowly grew from a penurious revolutionary exile into a freelance radical author and journalist.

In the summer of 1852, Marx started writing regular commentaries on European politics for the *New York Daily Tribune*. He started as an occasional contributor, and initially Engels— from Manchester—had to help with his English before he sent these dispatches by mail to New York. But slowly the pieces turned into almost weekly reports, and Marx was paid between three and five pounds per article. This was not sufficient for the Marx household's growing expenses, but it gave him some financial security. He continued writing these articles until 1862, most of them running commentaries on current affairs, but also some addressing wider issues with theoretical implications, as we shall see.

In the spring of 1856 Jenny inherited two considerable sums of money from her uncle, and later that year she received a further legacy from her mother's estate. Marx's own mother, who consistently refused to help her son financially, died in Trier in November 1863, and Marx—who was able to attend her funeral—received his share of her (and actually his father's) inheritance. This enabled the Marx family to move from the cramped quarters in Soho to a commodious house at 1 Modena Villas, Maitland Park, Hampstead.

At the same time one of Marx's closest colleagues in the League of Communists, Wilhelm Wolff, died in Manchester. An educator of independent means, he left Marx the considerable sum of eight hundred pounds. This made a major difference, extricating Marx from most of his debts, although, lacking a fixed income of his own, it did not solve all of his financial problems. Engels eventually settled on granting him a regular fixed sum of money. Eventually, the Marx family moved to another address in Hampstead, at 41 Maitland Park Road. Eleanor, their youngest daughter, was born in 1855.

RETHINKING THE REVOLUTION

After the failure of the revolutions of 1848 there was a distinct shift in the nature of Marx's writings. Hitherto, most of his writings were either philosophical treatises in the Young Hegelian vein, criticism of the existing order, polemics against fellow radicals, and attempts to lay the foundations of his economic thinking, or political brochures like the *Manifesto* published on behalf of groups he was associated with and which did not carry his name. After 1849 his most significant writings are detailed analytical studies of developments in specific countries— mainly France and Germany—trying to understand the reasons for the failures of the revolutionary waves—and hopes—of 1848.

The shift is not only from the philosophical and exhortative to the sociological, but also from the powerful world-historical generalities of the *EPM* and the *Manifesto* to the tedious quotidian details of political and social reality.

Because France was always the hope of the revolutionary left—and the home of its greatest disappointments—it is not surprising that Marx's two most seminal post-mortem essays dealt with French developments. The first was titled "The Class Struggles in France, 1848–1850," and the second was "The Eighteenth Brumaire of Louis Bonaparte." Both appeared in marginal publications and did not have much of an impact at the time. Yet in terms of Marx's own intellectual development, they provide a clear rethinking and to a large extent also signify the direction his own interests and preoccupations would move toward for the rest of his life.

"The Class Struggles in France" was published in four installments in four consecutive numbers of the *NRZ Revue* in 1850. It was republished with some emendations by Engels in Berlin in 1895, more than a dozen years after Marx's death. The introduction by Engels, written at the height of the growth of the German Social Democratic Party, aimed at a very different audience and largely overshadowed Marx's contemporaneous analysis of what had happened in France almost half a century earlier.

The very title of Marx's essay obviously raises the question of its relationship to the postulates of the *Manifesto* and clearly suggests a different historical paradigm. Whereas the *Manifesto* proclaimed a radical polarization of capitalist society into bourgeois and proletarians, with the eradication and proletarianization of all intermediary groups and social classes, the detailed study from 1850 suggests a very different picture of a complex, multilayered society, where many conflicting interests crisscross each other, bringing about shifting coalitions among multiple groups and subgroups and thus impeding the emergence of a clear-cut, polarized class warfare. It was this fractious nature of France's class structure that caused the failure of working-class insurrections in Paris during the summer of 1848, according to Marx. He also dwells on the relative strength of the conservative peasantry in the countryside and other traditional groups, which reasserted themselves during the revolutionary months—again very different from the prognosis of the *Manifesto* about the disappearance of the peasantry as a distinct class.

Without saying so explicitly, Marx clearly admits that the apocalyptic messages of the *Manifesto* of a modern Armageddon did not play out in 1848 and were, in fact, not accurate. This sober analysis is the intellectual background to his opposition in the early 1850s to the attempts of the radical wing of the League of Communists to have once again recourse to revolutionary activity: the failures of 1848 were structural, not accidental, and demanded rethinking.

Marx does, however, cushion his insights by defensive language. He starts the first article by maintaining that most accounts of 1848 talk about the defeat of the revolution, arguing that "what was brought low by these defeats was not the revolution—it was the pre-revolutionary traditional trappings, the result of social relationships which had not yet intensified to sharp class antagonisms." He goes on to suggest:

> Revolutionary progress forced its way not through its immediate tragicomic achievements, but conversely in creating a united and powerful counter-revolution, in creating an opponent, combat with whom brought the party of revolt to maturity as a true revolutionary party.

This is scant consolation, especially as the essays describe in great detail the failure of the revolutionary movement in France. To Marx's credit, one has to say that even at this early stage he was aware how the emergence of Louis-Napoleon created an unusual coalition of revolutionary rhetoric and conservative politics, which would show its resilience only some time later and which Marx would then describe with biting sarcasm and furious frustration in his "Eighteenth Brumaire" essay. Be this as it may, it is precisely the great length Marx goes to in the four articles describing the complexity of French society that shows that the polarization theory of the *Manifesto*—and the ensuing supposed radicalization of class struggle—did not play out as envisaged.

These complexities are then honestly and explicitly brought out by Marx in the "Eighteenth Brumaire of Louis Bonaparte." This article, published in 1852 after Louis-Napoleon had firmly established his rule, was printed in the German-language *Die Revolution* in New York, with even less visibility in Europe than the earlier four articles on the class struggles in France. Marx himself was well aware how little this essay was known in Europe, and under slightly more auspicious conditions he took care to issue a separate reprint in Hamburg in 1869, a short time before Napoleon III's ignominious defeat in the Franco-Prussian War and the collapse of his imperial rule. Engels edited a third printing in 1885, with his own introduction, which again tended to overshadow Marx's insights.

The strange title of the essay, referring to the date according to the French revolutionary calendar of the coup d'état of Napoleon I, is mainly etched in memory due to Marx's pithy statement in the opening paragraph that "all great incidents and individuals of world history occur twice—the first time as tragedy, the second as farce." The substance of the article is of course much more substantial than this reference to a statement Hegel is supposed to have uttered (although there is no evidence that he ever did).

Despite what may appear as a glib attempt to make Louis-Napoleon's ascent a target of sarcasm and irony, Marx takes his coming to power seriously. The essay follows the line Marx had taken a few years earlier in his articles describing the complexities of the class structure in French society. In an unusual insight, he characterized the appeal of Louis-Napoleon to different classes in France as typical of plebiscitarian, authoritarian rulers—in a way prefiguring later theories about the appeal across class lines of fascist and populist nationalist movements and leaders. The irony is that these very insights run, of course, contrary to Marx's theoretical premises that political power is a mere expression of economic interests: here he admits that the relationship between economic interests and political power is much more complex and not as simplistic or linear as he himself had maintained in the *Manifesto*.

But in this essay Marx also goes one step further regarding his assessment of the 1848 revolution in France. First of all, he criticizes the revolutionaries of 1848 for viewing themselves through the lens of historical memories of the French Revolution of 1789, bitingly commenting that they need "to strip themselves of all superstitions of the past." The social revolutions of the nineteenth century "cannot draw their poetry from the past but only from the future." This attempt to replay 1789 caused a misunderstanding of the present, Marx claimed, passing a far-reaching verdict on the 1848 revolutions, viewing them as mere episodes and not—as he himself did in the past—as turning points of history.

> The February revolution [of 1848] was a sudden attack taking the old society by surprise but the nation proclaimed this unforeseen stroke as an act of universal significance, inaugurating a new epoch.

Because the 1848 revolution was not such a structural, universal event, it was relatively easy for Louis-Napoleon to do away with it by appealing to the mixed coalition of social forces that saw him both as a deliverer and a bulwark. In a statement that would later figure strongly in various interpretations of

Marx's legacy, he introduced a nuance into his former theoretical views about how history is made by human beings. Human agency is the foundation of historical action, but this action is not done in an abstract way; it is always historically contextualized and therefore circumscribed.

> Men make their own history, but not at their own will under conditions they have chosen for themselves; rather it happens on terms immediately existing, given and handed down to them. The traditions of countless dead generations are an incubus to the mind of the living.

This pointing to the inextricable burden of history, which is different from country to country, is very different from the overall general statements of the *Manifesto*, and leads Marx in his further studies to look much more carefully at the diverse historical traditions of each society. Categories like "bourgeoisie" or references to general modes of production will have to be coupled with in-depth understanding of the peculiarities of each society—and this is how he explains the emergence of the unique phenomenon of Louis-Napoleon in the context of French history. Later this also led Marx to a differentiated prognosis of the conditions of a proletarian revolution in different European countries, and to a recognition of American exceptionalism, due to the availability of free land in the West.

The irony of this essay is that for all of his in-depth analysis of French social conditions, at the time he wrote it Marx imagined the ascendancy of Louis-Napoleon—later Emperor Napoleon III—would be short lived. At the end of the essay he predicts that the mantle of Napoleon will sit uneasily on the shoulders of his nephew Louis-Napoleon, and he was doomed to fail. Eventually he did, in 1871, but this occurred not as a result of internal tensions or upheavals. In any case, it took place almost twenty years after Marx published his essay.

SHIFTING VIEWS ON NATIONALISM

A much more subtle but no less far-reaching reassessment caused by the events of 1848 changed Marx's views on the role of nationalism and the emergence of national movements.

One of the main arguments of the *Manifesto* was the universalizing impact of capitalist industrial development: just as local, inward-looking traditional modes of production give room to the revolutionizing powers of the world market, so local, regional, and national differences disappear in the face of the emerging universal world culture.

This approach to nationalism was one of the issues on which Marx disagreed with his friend and colleague Moses Hess, who maintained that world history is the history not just of class warfare but also of national struggles. As early as 1843, Hess envisaged and supported Italian national unification. It was this approach that eventually also led Hess to call, in *Rome and Jerusalem: The Last Nationality Question*, from 1862, for the establishment of a Jewish socialist commonwealth in Palestine as the expression of Jewish national identity.

The events of 1848–49 caused Marx to change his position that nationalism is basically a pre-modern phenomenon, due to disappear under the impact of the world market. From his perch as editor of the *NRZ* in Cologne, he followed closely developments all over Europe and witnessed the forces of nationalism in Germany, Poland, Hungary, and the Czech lands. It turned out that the power of nationalism appeared in many cases stronger than Marx initially imagined, and much more decisive than the forces of the working class or of class conflict: insurrections in Prague and Budapest were fueled by national sentiments, not proletarian class consciousness. Moreover, nationalist consciousness trumped proletarian solidarity, and the statement in the *Manifesto* that "the proletarians have no homeland" turned out to be rather hollow.

Marx never stated explicitly that all this called for a reassessment. But his post-1848 positions on national independence and the movements for German and Italian unification showed a clear transformation. He obviously held to his position that the more capitalist and industrialized society became, the stronger the proletariat became; yet now a further dimension was added. If industrial capitalist development in regions like Germany and Italy was hampered by the existence of numerous small, separate states, each with its own separate laws, currency, and customs regulation, it would be critical to set up larger unitary markets in Germany and Italy that would do away with these impediments—and only political unification could bring this about. Large political entities—a unified Germany, a unified Italy—are therefore necessary for industrial capitalist development that would lead to the rise of a strong proletariat, enhancing the chances of a socialist revolution. Far from being a premodern phenomenon, national unification came to be viewed by Marx as part of modernity and a necessary condition for a future socialist society.

But there were of course nuances: nationalism was viewed by Marx not on its own intrinsic historical or cultural merits, but merely instrumentally, as the condition for creating large economic spaces. This meant that he tended to support the emergence of large national states—Germany, Italy—while being skeptical about the claims of smaller nations like the Czechs or some Balkan lands. This sometimes put Marx in the position of supporting large national claims, such as Germany's, while disregarding the attempts of smaller nations for self-determination: a problematic public and even moral stance. Some critics went so far as to label Marx a German nationalist, which is obviously nonsense. But one cannot avoid realizing that this position continued to haunt the socialist movement for decades and led to such divergent attempts to combine socialism and nationalism as Austro-Marxism, Leninism, and socialist Zionism.

Be this as it may, Marx no longer saw nationalism as a premodern phenomenon doomed to disappear before the juggernaut of what we would today call globalization. Without ever admitting it, Marx took a position on this issue that was closer to that of Moses Hess, though without recognizing—as Hess did—the value of the cultural dimensions of national movements as such. But realizing that nationalism is not just a pre-modern relic shows that Marx did internalize the lessons of 1848.

ON INDIA AND THE "ASIATIC MODE OF PRODUCTION"

Marx wrote for the *New York Daily Tribune* more than two dozen articles on British rule in India, some in the wake of the Indian Revolt of 1857, and some before it. Most are straightforward reports about current affairs, including scathing critiques of the brutality of the British suppression of the revolt. But two articles preceding the revolt stand out in addressing fundamental historical issues: "The British Rule in India" (published on 25th June 1853) and "The Future Results of British Rule in India" (8th August 1853). On these two occasions, Marx was able to integrate reporting on current affairs with his general views of world history.

It appears that Marx had very little sympathy with the immediate causes of the revolt: it was precipitated by the refusal of Hindu and Muslim soldiers in the British East India Company's army to open ammunition cartridges wrapped in animal fat by having to bite them with their teeth—an expression for him of the retrograde state of Indian society. For all of Marx's harsh criticism of British commercial and financial interests and policies in India, the revolt was not "The First Indian War of Independence," as later claimed by both the Communist movement and Indian nationalists: Marx viewed it through the dialectical prism of his general view of history, and if the upshot is somewhat paradoxical, it adds to the depth of his approach to historical developments.

Like many other aspects of his thought, Marx's views on India—and the non-European world in general—draw clearly on Hegel. In his *Philosophy of History*, Hegel referred to what he called "the Oriental Realm," which included not only ancient Egypt, Assyria, and Babylonia, but also contemporary India and China. According to Hegel, these "Oriental despotisms" are static societies, without internal mechanisms of change and hence, in a most fundamental way, outside the realm of history that Hegel identified as the march toward the consciousness of freedom. Such views, quite common among European thinkers since the writings of the seventeenth-century French traveler François Bernier, who is quoted frequently by Marx, were integrated by him into a wider philosophy of history that allots a unique dialectical role to European imperialism, economic and political.

In the two articles on India, Marx adds a socioeconomic dimension to what previous thinkers have called the static and stagnant nature of Asian societies. While all other forms of society—slaveholding, feudal, and capitalist—carry according to Marx their own economic and social internal dynamism of change, the static nature of Indian society precludes this. He even goes to the extreme, stating that "Indian society has no known history. What we call its history is but the history of the successive intruders who founded their empires on the passive basis of that unresisting and unchanging society."

The reason, according to Marx, for this unchanging nature of India—and Asian society in general—had already been identified by Bernier: "the absence of private property in land." The need to control water resources in extensive river valleys creates the unique nature of the "Asiatic mode of production." Marx elaborates:

> There have been in Asia, from immemorial times, but three departments of Government: that of Finance, or the plunder

of the interior; that of War, or plunder of the exterior; and, finally, the department of Public Works. Climate and territorial conditions, especially in the vast tracts of desert, extending from the Sahara, through Arabia, Persia, India and Tartary . . . constituted artificial irrigation by canals and waterworks the basis of Oriental economy.

This prime necessity of an economical and common use of water, which, in the Occident, drove private enterprise to voluntary association as in Flanders and Italy, necessitated in the Orient where civilization was too low and the territorial extent too vast to call into life voluntary associations, the interference of the centralizing power of Government. Hence an economical function developed upon all Asiatic Governments, the function of providing public works.

This to Marx is the economic basis of what emerged as Oriental despotism, based on village communities totally dependent on centralized government, which necessarily puts all land under its control.

Unlike many other European liberals and socialists—then and now—Marx shows no sympathy for the indigenous village communities of India being destroyed by the impact of English commercial and industrial activity. "I share not the opinion of those who believe in a golden age of Hindoostan," he said; against the idealizing picture sometimes painted by Western romantics, he gives a scathing account of the Indian village communities. The language is among the harshest used by a European observer:

> Sickening as it must be to human feeling to witness . . . these inoffensive social organizations disorganized and thrown into a sea of woes . . . we must not forget that these idyllic village communities, inoffensive as though they may appear, had always been the solid foundation of Oriental despotism, that they restrained the human mind within the smallest possible compass, making it the unresisting tool of superstition, en-

slaving it beneath traditional rules, depriving it of all grandeur and historical energies.

We must not forget the barbarian egotism which, concentrating on some miserable patch of land, had quietly witnessed the perpetration of unspeakable cruelties, the massacre of the population of large towns [as if these were mere natural disasters]. We must not forget that this undignified, stagnatory and vegetative life, that this passive sort of existence, evoked on the other part wild, aimless, unbounded forces of destruction, and rendered murder itself a religious rite in Hindoostan. We must not forget that these little communities were contaminated by distinctions of caste and by slavery, that they subjugated man to external circumstances instead of elevating man to be the sovereign of circumstances . . . and thus brought about a brutalizing worship of nature exhibiting its degradation in the fact that man, the sovereign of nature, fell down on his knees in adoration of Hanuman, the monkey, and Sabbala, the cow.

Reading this today, it is easy to condemn Marx for his European cultural hegemonism; yet it is equally justified to see in it a deep humanistic commitment, aware of the complex challenge of how to condemn British imperialistic brutality without falling into the pitfall of romantic idealization of the cruelties of pre-modern societies. The condemnation of Britain is clear and unequivocal, yet moral condemnation is a poor substitute for historical understanding, and it is here that Marx takes up the task of painting a wider canvas.

England has to fulfill a double mission in India: one destructive, the other regenerating—the annihilation of old Asiatic society, and the laying of the material foundations of Western society in Asia.

He then goes on to suggest how British rule has already transformed India and will continue to transform it in the wake of the suppression of the revolt.

The political unity of India, more consolidated and extending . . . than under the Great Moguls, was the first condition of its regeneration. That unity, imposed by the British sword, will now be strengthened and perpetuated by the electric telegraph. The Indian army, organized and trained by the British drill-sergeant, was the sine qua non of Indian emancipation, and of India ceasing to be the prey of the first foreign intruder. The free press, introduced for the first time into Asiatic society, and managed principally by the common off-spring of Hindoos and Europeans, is a new and powerful agent of reconstruction. The Zamindaree and Ryotwar themselves, abominable as they are, involve two distinct forms of private property in land—*the great desideratum of Asiatic society*. From the Indian natives . . . a fresh class is springing up, endowed with the requirements for government and imbued with European science [italics added].

And so it goes on and on. Eurocentric as it obviously is, this postulate is one of the most profound nineteenth-century analyses of the impact of Western imperialism on the Third World— and it spells out in detail what Marx described in the *Manifesto* as the revolutionizing role of the capitalist mode of production.

Yet all this is accompanied by an unequivocal condemnation of British interests in India, and his rhetoric equals his scorn: "The [British] aristocracy wanted to conquer it, the moneyocracy to plunder it, the millocracy to undersell it." But, he insists, "this is not the question." The question is that Britain is causing "a social revolution in Hindoostan." He then concludes:

Can mankind fulfil its destiny without a fundamental revolution in the social state of Asia? If not, what may have been the crimes of England she was the unconscious tool of history in bringing about the revolution.

It must have taken some moral courage to pass this judgment in the midst of the understandable revulsion among the

European and American democrats and socialists at the sight of the brutalities committed by the British in the course of putting down the Indian Revolt. Yet paradoxical as it may sound, the Indian Revolt served to validate Marx's world-historical analysis of capitalism, its discontent—and its crucial dialectical role in bringing about a worldwide socialist transformation.

7

The First International and Das Kapital

As Marx's financial situation gradually improved in the mid-1850s, he found it possible to concentrate more on his economic studies, though his need to provide almost weekly reports for the *New York Daily Tribune* and other papers still consumed much of his time. He also had health problems—intestinal complaints, boils, and other troubles—and these added to the family's expenses. The cures he had to undergo sent him to various spas, and he and his wife began spending time in resorts, both in England and then also on the Continent. As time passed, it also became clear that any hope of ever returning to Germany had evaporated, and attempts to regain his Prussian citizenship did not succeed.

The Marx family experienced the tensions of many émigrés who managed to gain some sort of economic comfort yet, deprived of a stable source of income or independent means, continued to live on a precipice. The Marxes were constantly burdened by debts, while at the same time making every effort to give their daughters language and music lessons and private tutoring, as befitting the children of what would be called in German the *Bildungsbürgertum* (academically educated middle class).

With three growing daughters, this was not an easy task for Marx. The surviving correspondence between father and daughters shows a warm and loving parent who, while insisting on their education, also introduced them to the thinking of the radical milieu the family moved in during their permanent London exile. All three daughters—Jenny, Laura, Eleanor—found husbands or partners, two of them French, who were involved in the democratic and socialist movement, and were themselves active to various degrees in politics and eventually also helped in publishing posthumously their father's oeuvre.

A glimpse into Marx's concern for his daughters as a responsible paterfamilias emerges from his letters concerning Laura's engagement to the young French socialist and medical student Paul Lafargue, then resident in London. Marx liked his future son-in-law, but the four years between the couple's engagement in 1864 and their marriage in 1868 are replete with concerns about their future financial situation. In letters to Lafargue Jr. as well as to his father back in France, Marx admonishes the young man first to finish his studies, and avoid for the time being political engagements: such activities, the worried future father-in-law claims, would be more effective when his professional standing was securely established. Marx also insisted on knowing exactly what sums Lafargue Sr. would commit himself to settle on the young couple. Marx obviously felt a bit uncomfortable with these typical bourgeois concerns, but in a revealing and moving letter to the older Lafargue he justified this by writing that he did not want his daughter to experience the same hardships and deprivations he himself had condemned his own wife and family to because of his political engagement.

These years also saw Marx's evolving ambivalent relations with Ferdinand Lassalle, who emerged in the early 1860s as the successful founder and charismatic leader of the first working-class mass movement in Germany—at a time when Marx was spending his days in the Reading Room of the British Museum, toiling away at his economic studies as well as gathering material for his newspaper dispatches to New York.

Lassalle's background was similar to that of Marx but also markedly different from it. He was born in 1825, the son of Heyman Lassal, a wealthy Jewish silk merchant in Breslau, in Prussia's southeastern province of Silesia. His father destined him to take over the family business, but the young Lassalle—who Frenchified the Jewish-sounding "Lassal" to "Lassalle"—rebelled and decided instead to study philosophy and law at Berlin University. Like many of his generation, he was deeply influenced by Hegelian philosophy, but while joining radical groups he did not forsake Hegel's insistence on the crucial role of the state in history and society—one of the future points of disagreement with Marx. He became associated with the League of Communists, but stayed out of trouble in 1848, remained in Germany, and was able after the failure of the revolution to live as an independent scholar supported by his family's wealth.

Lassalle published a number of serious—but little noticed—scholarly works on property rights and the dialectical philosophy of Heraclitus, but he gained fame—and notoriety—in the 1850s when as a lawyer he defended Countess Sophie von Hatzfeldt in a celebrated divorce and alimony litigation against her husband that lasted for years. Presenting his argument as a battle for a woman's rights in matrimony, he won the case—and the money—for the countess, who became his patron and, despite being twenty years his senior, also his companion. Her wealth helped to cushion his somewhat ostentatious lifestyle.

During the Prussian parliamentary crisis of the early 1860s, Lassalle succeeded in bringing together a number of radical and working-class groups, and in 1863 founded in Leipzig the General German Workers Association (ADAV). Using his considerable rhetorical powers and his public visibility as a celebrated popular lawyer who stood for a maligned woman, Lassalle succeeded in turning the ADAV into a mass movement—actually the first organized working-class mass party not only in Germany but in continental Europe. Through massive public rallies, often accompanied by his aristocratic companion, dramatic press pronouncements, leaflets and brochures, the ADAV quickly became a political force calling for universal suffrage, workers' rights and participation in the political process, with a strong emphasis on German unification. His support for universal suffrage created an implicit alliance with the Prussian prime minister Otto von Bismarck, who played with the idea as a way of circumventing the liberal middle-class parliamentary ascendancy in the Prussian Diet, which was elected through a limited, property-based suffrage. Bismarck and Lassalle held a number of meetings—an extraordinary event, and a strange alliance, evoking both support as well as extreme criticism. In his memoirs, Bismarck praised Lassalle with a backhanded compliment as "this clever Jew."

Lassalle's meteoric rise could only have been viewed with some ambivalence by Marx. On one hand, they differed on a number of issues, mainly Lassalle's attempt to forge a conservative-proletarian anti-bourgeois alliance, while Marx always believed in supporting—albeit critically—bourgeois claims so as to promote capitalist industrial development and thus strengthen the power of the proletariat, which would eventually overthrow bourgeois rule. On the other hand, Lassalle's phenomenal historical success in organizing a mass working-class movement was a major breakthrough that Marx could not overlook. The two corresponded frequently, Lassalle visited London and helped Marx financially, and he also introduced him to German-language democratic and socialist editors. Marx was obviously grateful and in a way beholden to him for this. Yet it was only natural that he viewed the success of the younger Lassalle with some reservation, and his lifestyle was not exactly what one would expect from a leader of a socialist movement.

In 1864, however, Lassalle was killed in an absurd duel with a Romanian nobleman, Janko von Racowitza, over a three-cornered romantic involvement with another noblewoman, Helene von Dönniges. The event only emphasized one of the bizarre aspects of Lassalle's life: nothing could be more outlandish than a socialist leader killed in a duel concerning an aristocratic lady.

Although Marx and Lassalle never allowed their differences to play out in public—and Marx could not really afford it, both personally and politically, as he was a relatively obscure émigré, compared with a successful political leader—some of his obvious frustration simmers to the surface in his correspondence. After a not very successful meeting in London in 1862, Marx reported to Engels about their disagreements, and then reverted to some crass and heavy-handed jocular language, a bit of ugliness that must have been compensation for his inner rage against a person he considered his intellectual inferior, who nonetheless provided the working class with an enormous organizational and political success. The fact that the comment came in a private letter—which decades later would embarrass many socialists, and Jewish socialists in particular—does not diminish its nastiness.

> It is now completely clear to me, as proved by the shape of his [Lassalle's] head and the growth of his hair, that he stems from the negroes who joined the march of Moses out of Egypt (if his mother or grandmother on his father's side did not mate with a negro). This combination of Judaism and Germanism with the basic negro substance must bring forth a peculiar product.

Even if one is accustomed to Marx's acerbic language about many other colleagues in the socialist movement who happened to disagree with him, this is particularly nasty, and shows how racist ideas were beginning to slip into the mainstream of European culture at that time, including the socialist movement. When Lassalle was killed in his bizarre duel, Marx and Engels exchanged comments about the utter stupidity and irresponsibility of it, yet Marx went on to praise Lassalle as one of the best and bravest in the working-class movement; his achievement could not be denied or gainsaid.

Marx's ambivalence toward Lassalle stands in contrast to his attitude toward another, even more prominent person of Jewish ancestry, Benjamin Disraeli. Despite obviously opposing his conservative politics, he had great admiration for Disraeli's political sagacity and statesmanship. In his articles and correspondence, Marx frequently refers positively to Disraeli's stark opposition to Russia, and his initiatives to expand the suffrage as well as introducing bills regulating working conditions—Tory steps that were opposed by the free-market liberals and echoed the young Disraeli's concern about Britain becoming "Two Nations."

In a letter to his Dutch uncle Lion Phillips in 1860, Marx playfully referred to Disraeli as *unser Stammgenosse* ("our tribesman" or "our tribal colleague"). Phillips was married to Marx's mother's sister, and went on to found the Phillips electrical firm. Like the Marx and Disraeli families, the Phillips family also converted to Christianity, so the allusion to a common consanguinity may have had more than one meaning, ironical or otherwise. Yet it is an aspect of his awareness of some common background (with Disraeli, of all people!) that Marx never expressed in a similar way in letters to colleagues and friends outside the family.

ON POLITICAL ECONOMY

A Contribution to the Critique of Political Economy [Zur Kritik der politschen Ökonomie] was Marx's first published major economic work, appearing in Vienna in 1859. Lassalle helped him find a publisher, although at the time the work had a very limited circulation (an English translation appeared only many years later, after Marx's death). Nonetheless, it was the first fruit of Marx's years-long economic studies, and in many ways foreshadowed *Das Kapital*. Because of its relatively compact form, it eventually became much more popular in the socialist movement than the lengthy, much more technical and comprehensive—and never finished—later work.

The structure of the work, as Marx announces in the preface, follows the main headings he sketched out in the *Economic-Philosophical Manuscripts* from 1844 and later repeated in *Das Kapital:* "I examine the system of bourgeois economy in the following order: capital, landed property, wage-labor, the state, world market"—an ambitious aim that he never fully accomplished. As already mentioned in Chapter 2, Marx recounts in the preface how he came to the study of political economy through the internal critique of Hegel's political philosophy; he further describes himself as "having studied jurisprudence subordinated to philosophy and history" and getting involved in "the embarrassing position of having to discuss what is known as material interests" as editor of the *Rheinische Zeitung*.

In mentioning some of the articles he wrote for the newspaper dealing with the link between economic interests and legislation as evidenced in the debates of the Rhenish Diet, he describes how this led him to reach his conclusions in the *DFJ* essays that legal relations and political forms cannot be understood without the study of "the material conditions of life, the totality of which Hegel, following the example of English and French thinkers . . . embraced in the term 'civil society,' and that the anatomy of this civil society has to be sought in political economy." He alludes to his beginning to study political economy in Brussels (the manuscripts eventually published by Engels as *The German Ideology*), but personal and political conditions made it impossible for him to conclude this work. He mentions the important contribution to the development of his theories made by the social and economic information provided by Engels in *The Condition of the Working Class in England* (1845), which supplied him with the necessary analytical and statistical data. This is a frank and honest admission by Marx that he never independently studied working-class conditions on his own. He sums up his conclusions in a passage that became the cornerstone of what could be called "historical materialism" (though he never adorned his theories with such a categorical definition).

> In the social production of their existence, men inevitably enter into definite relations that are independent of their will, namely relations of production appropriate to a given stage in the development of their material forces of production. The totality of these relations of production constitute the economic structure of society, the real foundation on which arises a legal and political structure and to which correspond definite forms of social consciousness. The mode of production of material life conditions the general process of social, political, and intellectual life.

He then concludes with a sentence that became canonical but has to be read carefully:

> It is not the consciousness of men that determines their existence, but their social existence that determines their consciousness.

This was a clear and radical repudiation of the whole tradition of German idealist philosophy from Kant to Hegel, although a caveat has to be added: in many references to this statement it is quoted as if what Marx said was: "it is existence that determines consciousness," suggesting that it is existence as such—physical, material—that determines consciousness. But Marx was not a crude materialist, and that is not what he wrote.

What he did write was that it is "*social* existence that determines consciousness." This includes a person's social position and relations to other persons: whether he or she is a worker or a property owner or a peasant. It is these *social* relations, and not merely material aspects, that determine the individual's consciousness; the social conditions of a worker, obviously, would have a different impact on consciousness from those of a peasant. It is for this reason that calling Marx's theory "historical materialism" takes into account his dialectical analysis of concrete social conditions, and does not limit itself merely to crass material elements in the physical world.

In a short description of historical developments, which transcends the rather dichotomic statements of *The Communist Manifesto*, Marx suggests that historical changes occur when there arise tensions between the economic structures of a given social order and its ideological superstructure. This is a much more nuanced and sophisticated approach to history than the simplistic—though highly powerful—opening statement of the *Manifesto* that "all history is the history of class struggles." In a further deviation from the polarization theories of the *Manifesto*, which describes capitalist society as characterized by a binary opposition between bourgeois and proletarians, Marx nevertheless clearly realizes the significance of landowning also in modern capitalist society, and planned to devote one of the six major sections of his study to it.

The preface also reflects Marx's internalization of the lessons of the failure of the 1848 revolutions. He does not say it explicitly, but the implication is obvious—in 1848 capitalist society was not yet developed enough to be overthrown and replaced by another mode of production.

> No social order is ever destroyed before all its productive forces for which it is sufficient have been developed, and new superior relations of production never replace older ones be-

fore the material conditions for their existence have matured within the framework of the old society.

And so as not to be misunderstood, he adds to this an admonition against utopian attempts to bring the End of Times prematurely, though this is couched in a beautiful, optimist language:

> Mankind thus inevitably sets itself only such tasks as it is able to solve, since closer examination will always show that the challenge arises only when the material conditions for the solution are already present or at least in the course of formation.

He then reiterates his long-held view that "the productive forces developing within bourgeois society create also the material conditions for a solution to its antagonisms." Hence the critical importance of understanding the inner mechanisms of capitalist society and monitoring its internal contradictions: this after all is the reason why Marx devoted his scholarly efforts to writing *Das Kapital*. This also explains his ferocious opposition to the radical insurrectionist views of the post-1848 remnants of the League of Communists and his later ambivalence toward the Paris Commune in 1871. In the 1860s this radical—though careful—strategy also determined the way he cooperated with the founders of the International Workingmen's Association and tried to steer its course.

THE INTERNATIONAL WORKINGMEN'S ASSOCIATION

The relative European stability of the late 1850s and early 1860s eventually reflected itself in the way the small radical groups in various countries—and their exiles, mainly in England—were rethinking their strategy. France was settling into the quasi-imperial conservatism of Napoleon III, Germany and Italy were moving, through a series of short local wars, toward unification, and Britain was able to overcome the Chartist challenge by its gradual evolution into a parliamentary democracy. Further industrial development constantly enlarged the working class, and defensive measures by the powers-that-be tried to mitigate the life conditions of workers so as to prevent radical outbursts. Prohibitions on union organizations were slowly being lifted, and some of the pre-1848 radical socialist leaders shifted to less revolutionary modes of activity. The success of Lassalle's movement in the German lands showed that violent revolution might not be the only path open to the growing numbers of industrial workers to achieve social and political aims.

It was in this atmosphere that the International Working-men's Association was founded in London in 1864. What was later to be called the First International grew out of meetings and rallies of international support for the failed Polish insurrection against Russian rule in 1863. These events brought together for the first time working-class activists from France and Britain, and out of these international contacts grew the idea of establishing some sort of coordinating body. In later socialist and communist historiography this was presented as the founding of an international revolutionary organization, with Marx at its center: it was nothing of the sort.

The initiative came from Owenites and remnants of the Chartist movement in Britain, and followers of Joseph Proudhon and Auguste Blanqui in France. The founding meeting took place at St. Martin's Hall in London on 18th September 1864, with the participation of representatives of British, French, German, Italian, Polish, Swiss, and Russian radical groups. The opening address was given by Professor Edward Spencer Beesly, who taught history at University College London. Fiery speeches against capitalism were made, but because of the heterogeneous composition of the founders—from supporters of the cooperative movement to anarchists and political revolutionaries—it was clear that the association would have to find a way to navigate among these tendencies and function basically as a coordinating correspondence society. An executive committee was elected, later to be called the General Council, and it elected an English shoemaker, George Odger, as its chairman. Later the council appointed a subcommittee to draft its program and rules.

Marx had no role in the founding of the IWA. He was invited to the founding meeting at St. Martin's Hall as a respected German émigré scholar, mainly through the initiative of some of his Chartist acquaintances. As he reported later to Engels in Manchester, he "sat as a mute figure on the platform," while the German refugee and tailor George Eccarius, a former member of the League of Communists, spoke on behalf of the London German Workers' Educational Association.

Yet this marginality was to change, when Marx was appointed by the General Council to the subcommittee tasked with drafting the IWA founding documents. The subcommittee held a number of meetings, some of them in Marx's house in Hampstead, and on 1st November adopted, with some changes, the drafts of both the formal inaugural address and the general rules proposed by Marx, preferring them to a number of other draft proposals offered by British and Italian members of the subcommittee.

The Inaugural Address of the General Council of the IWA, as well as its General Rules, were indeed drafted by Marx, but they were institutional documents of the IWA, not his personal writings: like *The Communist Manifesto*, they of course reflected Marx's views, but like every document drafted by a committee, they had to take into account the positions of other members, and in the IWA's case get the approval of the General Council. It was only later, in publications of the German SPD after Marx's death, and of course in the Soviet editions of Marx's writings, that these documents were presented as his personal writings and became part of the Marxist canon. Their status as institutional documents, not just Marx's own personal views, should not be overlooked.

This comes out very clearly in the Inaugural Address, which the General Council published as an official document in English and German, and was later published also in Italian and Russian.

The address starts with a typical Marxian description of the worsening life conditions of the industrial proletariat between 1848 and 1864. Contrary to the claims of bourgeois economists and politicians that economic development would alleviate the conditions of the proletariat, the address provided statistical data, based on Marx's own economic research later appearing in *Das Kapital*, that this was not the case: pauperization and polarization did continue, and the capitalist economy cannot solve its structural problems. As is Marx's method, much of the data come from parliamentary and other official publications.

Yet in a nod to those members of the IWA, mainly Proudhon and his followers, who focused on syndicalist trade union activity and the Owenite cooperative movement, the address mentioned two developments it called positive: the introduction in Britain of the Ten Hours Bill, which for the first time went beyond the free market model that opposed any state interference in employer-worker relations, and, second, the widening scope of the cooperative movement in Britain, which also limited the unbridled power of the market mechanisms of supply and demand.

At the same time, the address insisted that these developments, encouraging though they were, could not substitute for what it called, in clearly Marxian language, "the conquest of political power" by the proletariat. This aim, it argued, was now accepted by the workers and carried out in the "simultaneous revival of working-class parties in England, France, Germany and Italy." The aim of the IWA is to coordinate these efforts and encourage international cooperation between working-class parties. Given the federative nature of the IWA, which would be underlined in the General Rules, no overall policy recommendation was given, but it emphasized that without political activity, further labor laws would never be enacted. Recalling the founding background of the IWA in international solidarity with the Polish insurgents, the address—not surprisingly—ends with a scathing critique of the "barbarous" policies of Russia in both Poland and the Caucasus and calls for the development of a policy based on solidarity among the nations. A reference is also made to the raging American Civil War and the "infamous crusade for the perpetuation of slavery." It is a radical document, but it is careful not to call for a violent revolution.

The General Rules are a clear corollary of the address. The aim of the IWA is described as establishing "a central medium of communication and coordination between working-class societies"; it underscores the federative structure of the IWA, explicitly stating in rule number 11 that despite "the perpetual bond of fraternal cooperation" between the various member societies, all groups joining "will preserve their existent organizations intact." The aim of the IWA is defined as "the emancipation of working classes," as part of a movement to put an end to "servitude in all its forms and to all social misery, mental degradation, and political dependence."

This struggle, the rules maintain, is not local or national, but international, and that was the reason for the establishment of the IWA. In rule 7 it states that its aim will be achieved only by the organization of the proletariat as "a political party dedicated to insuring the victory of the social revolution as its ultimate aim—the abolition of all classes." The clear focus is on political organization: trade union activities and the establishing of cooperatives are important, but will not suffice.

Most of the rules deal with organizational issues: regular annual congresses, membership conditions, the role of the General Council and its procedures. The main function of the General Council is to exchange and disseminate information, and its operational decisions have to be approved by each member organization. Council activities have to conform to the law prevailing in each country; it is clear that the rules try to navigate carefully between the IWA's transformative goals ("social revolution") and not getting involved in illegal revolutionary activities, which could bring about new oppressive policies and lead once again to an 1848-like defeat. For good measure the rules also insist that all member organizations—and individual members—have to accept the principles of "truth, justice, and morality . . . in their conduct towards all men, without regard to color, creed, or nationality." This moralistic stipulation was obviously inserted at the insistence of members other than Marx. A few days later in November, the General Council instructed Marx to congratulate Abraham Lincoln on its behalf on his reelection as president of the United States.

The role of Marx in the IWA is significant but ambivalent: despite what later social democrats and communists maintained, he was neither its founder nor its leader, though as a member of the General Council he played a significant role in its history— mainly in crafting its documents, not necessarily in its decisions on political activity. That had to do with his unique position— undoubtedly the foremost socialist intellectual and scholar, but having no organized political movement behind him.

As a member of the General Council of the IWA, with its seat in London, Marx took part in all of its deliberations. As its corresponding secretary, he had a crucial role in establishing and maintaining the international network the IWA provided for various radical and democratic groups across Europe. With strong personalities like Giuseppe Mazzini and Mikhail Bakunin involved in its activities, it was unavoidable that internal disagreements reflected not only policy differences but also personal agendas stemming from the different goals, some of them nationalist in their origin, transcending issues of proletarian solidarity. The IWA supported the aims of the Irish national movement and identified Russia as the major enemy of all progressive forces in Europe. Being responsible for its international contacts, Marx signed many of its statements in his correspondence with various groups, but they were the outcome of institutional decisions of the IWA, not always identical with his own views, as can be seen from the records of the General Council's meetings. Disagreements over the pro-Bismarckian policies of the ADAV after Lassalle's death, as well as links between the French member groups of the IWA with Napoleon III's government, figure prominently in deliberations of the General Council. The built-in tension between the guaranteed autonomy of all member organizations and the wish of the General Council (usually supported by Marx) to project some centralized authoritative voice consumed much of the discussions and correspondence.

That Marx could not travel openly to the Continent because of his past record meant that he was unable to attend the IWA's founding congress in Geneva in 1866, as well as the subsequent congresses in Lausanne (1867), Brussels (1868), and Basel (1869). The only congress he did attend was in 1872, in The Hague, which—as we shall see—after the disaster of the Paris Commune practically led to the dismantling of the IWA when it decided to move its headquarters to the United States. Marx's absence from the congresses obviously kept him away from much of the decision-making process—and internal disagreements—characterizing the IWA's activities. Nevertheless, his involvement in its endeavors over several years was his most sustained direct participation in a working-class organization, and it left a voluminous paper trail due to his function as the association's corresponding secretary. Yet it has to be emphasized again and again that, contrary to later legend, Marx was not the towering leader of what was eventually celebrated as the first working-class international organization, with its historical role that became canonized by the name of the First International. Unlike the Second International, which represented massive socialist movements and parties in the years 1886–1914, the IWA was, for all its historical significance, a marginal organization made up of small and not very influential groups. At the time, it had little political impact, whereas the Second International became a major player in European politics.

Marx never finished his major economic study. His difficult life conditions obviously contributed to this failure, and his need to provide for years almost weekly reports to the *New York Daily Tribune* clearly interfered with his ability to concentrate on what he thought would be his magnum opus. But there is no doubt that there were also theoretical obstacles, not the least of them being how to reconcile his revolutionary ideology with attempting to write what should at the same time be a scholarly study that would not be brushed aside as just another political pamphlet. Engels was well aware of these difficulties, and in their correspondence he tried to push Marx to concentrate on his theoretical studies: much of the generous financial support he provided for years was aimed at this goal, so as to free Marx from hack work. Occasionally he even chided Marx, which must have been slightly upsetting; in a letter of February 1860 he gently asked: "What will it help us . . . if even the first volume of your book will not be ready for publication when we shall be surprised by events?" Marx did not respond to this taunt.

From Marx's voluminous drafts it becomes clear that he did not give up his ambition to write a comprehensive work, of which *Das Kapital* would be just the first of six volumes; this would be followed by volumes on landed property, wage labor, the state, foreign trade, and the world market. This was of course an impossible mission, and during his lifetime Marx was unable to follow up the publication of *Das Kapital*, volume 1. Some of Marx's manuscript notes were published later by Engels as volumes 2 and 3.

Volume 1 was published in Hamburg under the title *Das Kapital—Kritik der politischen Ökonomie*, and in choosing this title Marx clearly indicated the audience to which he was aiming. Like the earlier *Contribution to the Critique of Political Economy* in 1859, this was not an exhortative call for a proletarian revolution but an attempt to reach a wider educated audience and instill into the scholarly and public discourse an internal, dialectical critique of modern capitalism. The book has to be judged as such, and this shift from a propagandistic revolutionary call aimed at political activists added of course to some of the intrinsic difficulties Marx had in finding the right calibration for his extensive study.

This also reflects Marx's post-1848 conviction that the eventual socialist transformation of society will not necessarily come about through a violent revolution but will be an outcome of the inevitable internal changes brought about by the tension inherent in the very development of capitalism itself.

What Marx was attacking was the very foundation of the leading ideas of the Adam Smithian free market ideology, and hence most of his criticism is aimed at the conceptual mechanisms underlying industrial capitalism. As a consequence, the book is a difficult read, and in his introduction Marx admitted to the density of his argument. To use contemporary language: Marx was aiming at deconstructing the conceptual grid through which capitalist society was presenting itself, and by insisting on the term "*political* economy," he was arguing that what was being presented as objective, eternal and scientific economic laws was nothing else than a human, social construct, determined by the agency of human development as evident in a concrete historical situation.

The titles of the various chapters attest to this: Commodities, Exchange, Transformation of Money into Capital, Surplus Value, and so on. In the first chapter, on commodities (which Marx acknowledged was the most abstract and theoretical part of his work), he insists on its multifaceted nature by pointing out the difference between use value and exchange value; he later goes on to analyze the commodification of human labor inherent in the capitalist mode of production and the way surplus value is the rock on which capitalist profit is based. All of these arguments have been made by Marx in some of his earlier writings, both published as well as left in manuscript form.

His core argument is repeatedly stated: despite the harmonistic "hidden hand" claim of classical economics, it is the inherent tensions and contradictions of capitalism that make it progressively unable to sustain itself through self-correcting mechanisms. Moreover, by presenting the forms of exchange as anchored in quasi-natural, deterministically formulated laws, capitalism abstracts from the basic fact that its mode of production is an outcome of human, historical development. By claiming this, classical economic theory is depriving humanity of its control over its actions: commodities are not objective natural phenomena, but human artifacts.

Yet beyond the purely economic analysis, *Das Kapital* (as well as the preparatory notes eventually published as *Grundrisse*) continues to echo some of Marx's earlier philosophical writings, though the arguments are presented in a more economically oriented language.

This relates primarily to the way Marx now addresses the issue of alienation, which has figured so prominently in his earlier writings. Given the fact that the term "alienation" had been used by other Young Hegelians in connection with spiritual themes and became sometimes identified with mere religious and psychological phenomena, Marx was careful to distinguish himself from these generalized and undifferentiated assertions and refrained from using the term in later writings; but he returns to this phenomenon in a different language. What was philosophically postulated in the *EPM* of 1844 is verified here and vindicated by an analysis of political economy in the discussion of commodities. A commodity, Marx argues, "is in the first place an object outside of us"; but on closer inspection, it appears as the objectified expression of subjectivity—of human labor. It is in this context that Marx develops his theory of the "Fetishism of Commodities," which is trying to express in economic terms the meaning of alienation.

In a lengthy paragraph, Marx argues that "a commodity is a mysterious thing, simply because in it the social character of men's labor appears to them as an objective character. . . . In the same way the light from an object is perceived by us not as the subjective excitation of our optic nerve, but as the objective form of something outside the eye itself." This, to Marx, is analogous to the mysteries of religion.

> In that world the productions of the human brain appear as independent beings endowed with life and entering into relations both with one another and with the human race. So it is in the world of commodities with the product of men's hands. This I call the Fetishism which attaches itself to the products of labor . . .

Human artifacts are then, according to Marx, presented by classical political economy as ruled by eternal laws to which human beings are subservient, while in truth they are merely an expression of human activity and therefore depend on human agency as part of human autonomy as producers. This deconstruction of the objective nature of commodities and economic laws is at the root of Marx's critique of the capitalist mode of production: it is not a law of nature, but open to human will and agency.

Recognizing this, and acting upon this recognition, will later be cited by Marx as opening the way to different paths of development in different capitalist societies, despite their similar stages of development. In a significant but somehow neglected passage in *Das Kapital*, Marx argues that in England there is a distinct possibility for the working class to reach power peacefully, not only because of the extension of the suffrage, but also due to various aspects of factory and social legislation, adding that "for this reason . . . I have given so large a space in this volume to history, details, and the results of English factory legislation." He also mentions the impact of the educational factory system introduced by Robert Owen's philanthropic experiments that show "the germs of the education of the future . . . that would combine productive labor with instruction and gymnastics . . . as the only method of producing fully developed human beings"—clearly echoing measure 10 of the Ten Regulations envisaged in *The Communist Manifesto*. The role of religious groups advocating ameliorating working conditions in factories is also pointed out.

Despite his reluctance to dabble in what to him would always appear as utopian fantasies as to how a future communist society would look, Marx does provide some suggestions about it even in a study obviously devoted to the working of the capitalist mode of production. These appear in some of his draft notes, which Engels published later, after Marx's death, as volume 3 of *Das Kapital*. Insisting as he always did that the transition to socialism—whether violent or peaceful—would have to go through a number of stages, Marx adds:

> In fact that realm of freedom actually begins only where labor which is determined by necessity and mundane considerations ceases . . . and thus lies beyond the sphere of actual material production. . . . The realm of physical necessity expands as a result of man's wants, but at the same time the forces of production also increase. Freedom in this field can consist in socialist man as the associated producers rationally regulating their interchange with Nature; bringing it under their common control, instead of being ruled by it as by the

blind force of Nature, and achieving this with the least expenditure of energy and under conditions most favorable to, and worthy of, their human nature.

To Marx socialism is inextricably bound with *Homo faber*'s transformation of nature and controlling it, not the other way round.

It is obvious that for generations *Das Kapital* was much more referred to—and attacked—than read in its entirety. Yet it gave the working-class movement a canonical text that presented the socialist case in a learned and theoretical way, beyond mere rhetoric and propaganda. It is doubtful that many people joined the socialist—or later communist—movement because they had read *Das Kapital* or could follow its arguments; but it helped make Marx's thought part of the public discourse of modern societies. It never supersedes such powerful texts as *The Communist Manifesto*, but it granted, especially to intellectuals who joined the socialist movements and styled themselves Marxists, a theoretical foundation for their critique of capitalism.

The publication of the first volume of *Das Kapital* also took place at a relatively propitious time, as it coincided with the slow but steady growth in many European countries of working-class parties that started playing a role in the political discourse of their respective societies. Within a few years, a number of translations would appear: somewhat surprisingly cleared by czarist censorship, a Russian translation was published in St. Petersburg in 1872, and a French version in 1872–75, supervised by Marx himself; following Marx's death, an Italian edition appeared in 1886 and an English one in 1887. All of this helped make Marx's name and reputation known, albeit modestly, beyond the narrow confines of the working-class movement, and it certainly did extricate him from his relative obscurity, even among people who never read the book or could really follow its arguments.

DARWIN—AND PROMOTING *DAS KAPITAL*

The analogy between Marx and Darwin had been made frequently, and it happens to be one of the few issues on which such disparate interpreters of Marx as Karl Kautsky and V. I. Lenin seemed to agree. The almost canonical comparison comes from the funeral oration Engels gave at Marx's grave on 17th March 1883:

> Just as Darwin discovered the law of development of organic nature, so Marx discovered the law of development of human history.

Engels repeated this analogy in his introduction to the English edition of *The Communist Manifesto* published in 1888, and the former companion of Marx's daughter Eleanor, Eduard Aveling, himself a biologist, reinforced it in his brochure *Charles Darwin and Karl Marx—A Comparison* in 1897. It then became a subject of numerous publications, among both Marxists and anti-Marxists: Marxists clung to it for the scientific legitimacy it apparently gave to Marx's thought, and anti-Marxists viewed it as a corroboration of the ungodly alliance between Darwinian evolutionists and socialist revolutionaries.

Yet Marx's own views on Darwin were much more ambiguous, and the correspondence between Marx and Engels shows very different approaches to Darwin. The analogy itself has a complex and even amusing origin connected with Marx's attempts to promote *Das Kapital.*

When volume 1 of *Das Kapital* was published in Hamburg in 1867, Marx was virtually unknown in Germany outside the small circle of pre- and post-1848 radical groups; with a short exception during 1848–49, he had not lived in Germany for a quarter century. Marx and Engels devoted considerable efforts to have reviews of the book published, and during 1867–68 Engels himself published nine reviews of *Das Kapital,* some under his own name, some under the name "F. Oswald" as well as other pseudonyms. Their aim was to present the book as a serious economic study, not a mere revolutionary screed. One of these reviews had an unusual background.

From the Marx-Engels correspondence it appears that an editor of a liberal south German newspaper, *Der Beobachter*, published in Stuttgart, contacted Engels with a request for a review. It seems that the editor did not know much about Dr. Marx, and heard that a German industrialist from Manchester had been writing reviews of the book and hence approached him with a request for a review article for his paper. Marx found out that the editor was a great admirer of Darwin and viewed his theory of biological "survival of the fittest" as legitimating a free-for-all market competition. Marx saw this as a wonderful opportunity to insert a favorable review of his book in a mainstream bourgeois German newspaper and advised Engels accordingly.

In a lengthy letter to Engels on 7th December 1867, Marx suggested how to present his book to a middle-class German audience. Much of this is written tongue in cheek, and reflects how eager Marx was to have his book reach a wider audience. Knowing that south German liberals were nationalists and anti-Prussian, Marx started by suggesting that Engels might present "Dr. Marx" and his work as "honoring the German spirit and therefore written by a Prussian living in exile and not in Prussia . . . since Prussia now represents the Russian, not the German, spirit." After this bow to German nationalism, Marx recommended that Engels write that one could disagree with the author's political "tendencies" while still agreeing with his "positive" scholarly analysis.

Aware of the Darwinist inclinations of the newspaper's editor, Marx proposed that Engels claim that the author,

> in showing that from an economic point of view, present society is pregnant with a higher form, he proves from a social

perspective the same gradual process of change proved by Darwin in the natural sciences. This is implied in the liberal theory of progress. It is the author's achievement in pointing out a hidden progress even when it is accompanied by immediate terrible consequences linked to modern economic conditions. In this the author, perhaps against his own will, puts an end to all professional socialism, that is utopianism . . .

Marx concluded his letter by saying that "this is a way to fool the Swabian philistine editor, and despite the fact that this swinish newspaper is small, it is the oracle of all federalists in Germany, and has also readers abroad."

Engels was happy to accept Marx's suggestions, and wrote a review that appeared in *Der Beobachter* three weeks later, on 27th December 1867. It follows Marx's concept, and more than thirty lines are lifted verbatim from Marx's letter, including the statement that one should make a distinction between the author's political tendencies and the positive methodology of his economic analysis. The reference to Darwin is explicit, though the denigration of "all socialists" is toned down a bit:

> Insofar as Marx tries to prove that from an economic point of view, present society is pregnant with a higher social form, he tries to transfer to the social sphere as a law the same universal process of change whose existence has been proved by Darwin in the natural science. . . . One has to point to Marx's achievements, since in contrast to other socialists, he points out progress even when it is immediately accompanied by terrible consequences. . . . In this, the author provided, probably against his own will, the strongest arguments against all professional socialists. . . .

One can see how far Marx and Engels were ready to go (and how desperate) to get attention to what Marx justly saw as his major contribution to economic thought—*Das Kapital*.

This is how Marx's quite sophisticated *jeu d'esprit*—which

he obviously enjoyed enormously—became the cornerstone of Engels's funeral statement, which became almost an epitaph. Whether Engels remembered the origins of the analogy when he made it, this time seriously, more than fifteen years later, is an open question. What is not in question is that Marx's own views on Darwin were, however, quite different.

Engels, with his general inclination toward the natural sciences, occasionally praised Darwin in his letters to Marx, yet Marx was much more skeptical. When Engels repeated his admiration for Darwin's scientific method, Marx, on at least one occasion, maintained that ultimately Darwin saw in nature only a reflection of the brutal competitive characters of bourgeois society. In a letter he wrote to Engels on 18th June 1862, he put it bluntly:

> Darwin, whom I have looked up again, amuses me when he says he is applying Malthusian theory also to plants and animals. . . . It is remarkable how Darwin recognizes among beasts and plants his English society with its division of labor, competition, opening up of new markets, "inventions" and the Malthusian "struggle for existence." It is Hobbes's *bellum omnium contra omnes* [war of all against all], and one is reminded of Hegel's *Phenomenology*, where civil society [*bürgerliche Gesellschaft*] is described as a "spiritual animal kingdom," while in Darwin the animal kingdom figures as civil society.

Far from seeing the theory of evolution as a serious scientific account, Marx considered it merely a mirror image of Darwin's own capitalist English society. A harsher verdict can hardly be imagined.

This is not the only instance where Marx compared Darwin's theory to an ideological reflection of bourgeois capitalist society. In a letter of 5th December 1868 to Ludwig Kugelmann, one of his correspondents in Germany, Marx criticized the biologist Ludwig Büchner, who praised Darwin and Darwinism, castigating him for making faulty analogies between biological and social development. This did not prevent Büchner from publishing a brochure in 1894 titled *Darwinismus und Sozialismus*, which was translated into many languages and helped to propagate the analogy between Darwin and Marx.

Marx repeated this criticism in another letter to Kugelmann, on 27th June 1870, this time against another German natural scientist, Friedrich Albert Lange, who published a book on social history "from a Darwinist perspective." Marx called it a rehash of old Malthusian ideas, characterizing the work as "blown-up, arrogant, quasi-scientific and lazy thinking."

There is a further twist to all this, which is sometimes misinterpreted in the light of Engels's funeral oration. At one time Marx considered dedicating *Das Kapital* to Darwin, and contacted him in this connection. This was obviously not because he admired his theories, but precisely because Darwin was an example of how capitalist reality was impacting scientific research. Darwin declined the honor—not, as some observers maintained, because he did not want to be associated with a revolutionary like Marx, but because he saw through the irony, if not sarcasm, of Marx's request.

Because of its catchy appeal, Engels's analogy between Marx and Darwin gained authoritative status. Its origin in a literary publicity joke is almost totally unknown, as are Marx's own devastatingly critical remarks about Darwin. This may not be the only case where funeral encomia distort historical memory.

8

◆◆◆◆

The Paris Commune and the Gotha Program: Debacle and Hope

THE PUBLICATION of *Das Kapital* as well as his role in the General Council of the International Workingmen's Association, responsible for much of its international correspondence, gave Marx a measure of public standing in London and abroad. The IWA became a vehicle for developing working-class solidarity across national boundaries, and although it never gave up its radical goals, it was clear that it was aiming at a gradual but fundamental transformation of society based on the growing power of working-class parties.

Marx's growing public visibility enabled him to take positions on wider issues of European politics, beyond the narrow confines of the IWA, and thus become, albeit in a modest way, part of the general public discourse in Britain.

One of the themes Marx addressed repeatedly was the role of Russia in European politics, and some of his writings in the

1860s discussed this issue. The immediate cause was Britain's involvement in the Crimean War against Russia; but for Marx there was a more fundamental reason for his wary attitude toward Russia, which later also drove him to speculate on the possibilities for a radical social revolution in Russia.

Marx's point of departure was his realization of the role Russia had played, since its involvement in the defeat of Napoleon, in international politics as the so-called "gendarme of Europe." This was greatly enhanced by Russia's role as a European power due to its control of most of the historical Polish-Lithuanian Commonwealth since the three partitions of Poland in the late eighteenth century, which was reconfirmed at the Congress of Vienna. That was the cause for Marx's support for Polish independence, which would both weaken Russia and put a distance between it and Europe proper. To Marx, each of Russia's interventions in European politics helped to defeat revolutionary movements and strengthened Europe's reactionary governments.

Marx was always ambivalent about the role of Napoleon in European politics and history: on one hand, his authoritarian imperial regime had put an end to the emancipatory vision of the French Revolution. Yet by bringing down the old absolutist and feudal order in many European countries—for Marx the memory of the liberating impact of French rule on the Rhineland was always present—Napoleon helped institutionalize some of the modernizing and even liberalizing legacies of the French Enlightenment. The defeat of Napoleon with the active help of Russia not only brought back the Bourbons to the French throne, but opened the door to the Restoration and the reactionary, counterrevolutionary coalitions of the so-called Holy Alliance headed by Metternich.

Similarly, Russia's intervention in the revolutions of 1848 in the Habsburg empire helped suppress the revolutionary movements in Budapest, Prague, and Vienna, and its repeated suppression of Polish insurrections also solidified the conservative monarchies of Prussia and Austria-Hungary. Marx's concern was that this might not augur well for future European revolutions: Russia could always side with reactionary European governments again, and thus stymie the revolutionary potential in central and even western Europe. If Russian troops reached Paris in 1814 and helped set up the post-1815 conservative Concert of Europe, the same thing could happen again. Hence, in some of his writings Marx found himself somewhat uncomfortably siding with conservative British politicians who saw the containment of Russia as one of their major geopolitical aims.

"THE MOST VILIFIED MAN IN LONDON"

What ultimately sidetracked these apprehensions was the outbreak of the Franco-Prussian War in the summer of 1870 as part of Bismarck's drive for the unification of Germany under Prussian hegemony. The war thrust the IWA—and Marx—into a vortex of totally unpredicted turmoil. It was impossible not to take a position on the war, and this became a tough challenge as the two largest sections of the association were the German and French ones; hence its main goal was to try to prevent the breakup of the IWA over the enmity and national tensions created by the war.

Two addresses issued by the General Council during the war—on 23rd July and 8th September 1870, were both drafted mainly by Marx, and bear witness to the challenges facing the IWA under the circumstances. The first address, written when the outcome of the war was still not clear, insisted that whatever happened, the most important goal for the IWA was to preserve the international solidarity of the working class and not allow chauvinism on either side to detract its national sections from the common aim of strengthening socialist parties and promoting the economic and social interests of the proletariat. Beyond this language of solidarity, however, it was clear that the IWA would welcome the downfall of the Second Empire of Napoleon III—not only because the emperor's belligerent diplomatic stance had triggered the war, but also because it viewed what Marx had called the "faux empire," with its attempt to gain popularity through its use of the Napoleonic myth, as a stumbling block toward a clear definition of class interests within French society that would greatly enhance the power of the working class.

This was not an easy position to take, as it tacitly implied support for Bismarck's drive for German unification under Prussia's hegemony. But it was here that Marx's historical analysis prevailed. As we have seen, after 1848, Marx viewed the creation of large nation-states as a precondition for intensive capitalist industrialization that would lead to the emergence of a strong working class crucial for eventual socialist transformation. So while not explicitly supporting a Prussian victory, the first address welcomed the downfall of Napoleon III. At the time, and subsequently, this caused some of Marx's opponents in the IWA to brand him as a Prussian and a German nationalist.

The IWA's second address, released within a week of the French defeat at the Battle of Sedan on 1st–2nd September 1870 and Napoleon's abdication, welcomed these developments, though without celebrating the German victory. It called upon the French workers to support the newly created republican provisional government and warned that "any attempt to upset the government of the French Republic in the present crisis will be a desperate folly."

Again, this was not an easy position to take, and developments moved in a completely different way. The ensuing emergence of the Paris Commune, which rebelled against the newly established bourgeois republican government, had a far-reaching impact on the IWA and to a large extent doomed it. Strangely and paradoxically, it also pushed the name of Marx into wide public visibility for the first time in an unprecedented and unforeseen way.

After the brutal defeat and suppression of the Commune, Marx's account of it—*The Civil War in France*, published in May 1871—became one of the classics of socialist and communist thought, and contributed to identifying him publicly with the movement, even though he had never advocated in favor of the insurrection.

A terminological serendipity was also involved. For historical reasons, the official name of the municipal government of the City of Paris was *Commune de Paris* (a similar echo of such medieval nomenclature is still evident in the name of the British House of Commons). This has nothing to do with communism, nor did the Commune carry out a communist or socialist platform. But its very name enabled later generations of Marxists—especially in the Soviet Union—to link Marx with an event that was very different in its historical context from the way it was later presented in left-wing ideology and propaganda.

As noted, Marx was instrumental in drafting the 8th September second address of the IWA, welcoming the abdication of Napoleon III, expressing support for the new republic, and warning against undermining it through radical acts. Yet not all members of the French section of the IWA, in exile in London, went along with this approach. These divisions between the IWA leadership and some of the French radicals are echoed in a letter Marx wrote to Engels on 6th September, reporting about the travel of an IWA official emissary, Auguste Serailler, to Paris:

> Serailler just comes in and informs me that he is leaving London for Paris tomorrow ... to settle the affairs of the International. . . . This is now even more necessary, since the whole French Branch [of the IWA in London] escapes now to Paris in order to do there all kinds of follies in the name of the International. They wish to bring down the Provisional

Government, to establish a Commune de Paris, nominate
Pyat French ambassador to London etc.

The people Marx was referring to were the followers of
Auguste Blanqui—the same radical group Marx had opposed
during the last days of the League of Communists after 1848.
He viewed them as irresponsible putschists, as he had judged
them to be in the early 1850s. Felix Pyat, a journalist and dra-
matist, was a veteran of the revolutionary phase of the 1848
French revolution, who on returning to France joined the Paris
Commune and took up a military command under its authority;
having no military experience, he led his unit to a disastrous defeat. He was exactly the kind of "alchemist of the revolution"
Marx had warned against in the 1850s.

Yet developments in Paris were well beyond the ability of
the IWA in London to control, and the emergence of the Paris
Commune and its insurrection against the republican government became one of those romantic, hopeless historical aber-
rations that nevertheless turned into historical icons—not least
because of Marx's lengthy essay following its defeat.

With the Prussian victory over the French imperial forces
and Napoleon III's dramatic abdication, France was thrown into
an almost unprecedented turmoil: a provisional government
under the veteran conservative politician Adolphe Thiers was
set up, seeking to reach an accommodation with the Prussians;
radical forces in the capital proclaimed themselves the Paris
Commune, refusing to accept the authority of the newly established republic; they were supported by a quickly assembled
municipal National Guard, which intended to continue to fight
the German invaders. Tragically they found themselves fighting not the Germans but the provisional government, with its
seat in Bordeaux and later in Versailles. Between 18th March
and 28th May 1871 the Paris Commune defended itself fiercely,
but what had started as a patriotic defense of the homeland

ended as a bloody and hopeless civil war. At the end the be-sieged Commune was defeated by the provisional government, with the tacit support of the victorious Germans. In order to further humiliate France, Bismarck orchestrated the crowning of the king of Prussia as German emperor on 18th January 1871 in the Versailles Palace Hall of Mirrors.

The suppression of the Commune was horribly cruel. After the government army succeeded in occupying Paris, more than 6,500 Communards were buried in mass graves, tens of thousands were taken prisoner, many of whom were jailed and deported. The wounds left by the Commune and its suppressions continued to haunt French politics for decades.

From London, Marx followed the agonizing developments, and even though he thought the insurrection was folly, he obviously could not support its brutal suppression. During the late winter and spring months of 1871 he prepared a number of drafts about the composition and history of the Commune, which served him when he wrote *The Civil War in France* following the Commune's defeat.

Yet there is a fundamental difference between the drafts and the final published essay. In the drafts Marx tries to identify the social structure of the Commune and its political aims, and concludes that it was basically a lower-middle-class affair, with scant proletarian input. In the published version, which heroically praises the Commune after its defeat, nothing of this appears. Furthermore, while the drafts are Marx's own conclusions about the Commune's social structure and represent his personal views, the text of *The Civil War in France* was issued and distributed as an official address of the General Council of the IWA and reflected its position in view of the brutal repression of the Commune by the conservative provisional government. The drafts were first published in the 1930s in an obscure Soviet journal and have been largely overlooked until now, while *The Civil War in France* has appeared for decades in all editions

of Marx's *Selected Works* as part of his canon. Engels's republica-
tion of it in 1891 as part of Marx's theoretical legacy was accompanied by his own introduction, which totally ignored Marx's
rather ambivalent approach to the Commune as expressed in
the drafts.

Marx's drafts clearly and unequivocally identify the rising
of the Commune with its petty-bourgeois leadership, and note
in great detail the immediate circumstances of the insurrection.
During the growing tension between the provisional government in Versailles and the Commune, which controlled Paris,
Versailles proclaimed a provisional moratorium on all outstanding bills of payments and rents. The aim of this moratorium was
obvious—to get the support of the lower middle class, mainly
in Paris, for Versailles, and for a time it worked. The moratorium was to expire on 13th March 1871, and representatives of
Paris middle-class associations tried to press for its extension,
but the provisional government in Versailles under Thiers refused. Marx recounts that between 13th and 18th March more
than 150,000 demands for payment of bills and rents were re-
activated, and then on 18th March the insurrection of the Commune broke out. Marx goes on to note that the demand for a
further, or definite, extension of the moratorium—obviously an
interest of lower-middle-class groups—continued to figure as
a major plank of the Commune. The drafts also contain further
analysis of the social structure of the Commune leadership,
pointing to its petty-middle-class composition.

Nothing of this appears in the published text of *The Civil
War in France*, which focused on the brutality of the Commune's suppression and on criticizing the policies of the Thiers
government. Obviously the initial support of the IWA for the
provisional government could not be maintained after the insurrection of the Commune took place, and hence the IWA—
and Marx—found themselves praising the idea of the Commune, even though they had initially opposed its very creation

and its refusal to accept the legitimacy of the provisional government. The text of *The Civil War in France* thus became both a testimony to the heroism of the Commune against the forces of reaction and a possible nonstate model for the structure of a socialist society of the future. Lenin used it repeatedly in his writings after 1917 to legitimate Soviet power as part of the legacy of Marx's teaching.

Yet a careful perusal of the text of *The Civil War in France* does reveal Marx's ambivalence. Although none of his views that the Commune was a lower-middle-class and not a proletarian affair appear in the published text, he nevertheless refrains from stating that it was a proletarian uprising. But when discussing the institutional arrangements envisaged by the Commune—which were never carried out in reality due to its short time of existence and eventual downfall—Marx sees in them a potential for a possible future society, despite the fact that they were never carried out. The text as published is in English, and one should note how Marx uses the conditional and subjunctive to describe what these institutions could mean. Had the Commune survived (which Marx never believed it would or could, yet obviously did not say so publicly), its arrangements— mainly the devolution of power from the highly centralized French state to the communal, municipal level, would be "a model for all the great industrial centers of France." He then goes on to give a few examples (italics are added to highlight the conditional):

> The communal regime *once established* in Paris and secondary cities, the old centralized Government *would* in the provinces, too, *have to give way* to the self-government of the producers. In a rough sketch of national organization *which the Commune had no time to develop*, it states clearly that the Commune *was to be* the political form of even the smallest country hamlet, and that in the rural districts the standing army *was to be replaced* by a national militia, with an extremely

short term of service. The rural communes of every district *were to administer* their common affairs by an assembly of delegates in the central town, and these district assemblies *were again to send* deputies to the National Delegation in Paris, each delegate *to be at any time revocable and bound* by the mandat imperative (formal instruction) of his constituents. The few but important functions which still *would* remain for a central government *were not to be suppressed*, as has been intentionally mis-stated but *were to be discharged* by Communal, and therefor strictly responsible agents. The unity of the nation *was not to be broken*, but on the contrary, *to be organized* by the Communal Constitution and *to become* a reality.

These are moving and powerful words of consolation and hope at the moment of defeat. They refer, however, not to what the Commune was, but only to what it could have been had it survived.

Marx's conviction that the Paris Commune was not a working-class insurrection and his general skepticism about its chances can also be gleaned from his correspondence with Leo Fränckel, the only member of the IWA in the leadership of the Commune. Fränckel was a Hungarian Jewish socialist who had spent years in Germany and later in France and was involved in Lassalle's movement. He was appointed public works commissioner by the Commune, and on 27th April 1871 asked Marx in a letter what steps he would suggest he should undertake. Marx responded on 17th May in the waning days of the Commune, and his letter shows once more how ambivalent he was about the Commune. While expressing support for its valiant resistance to the forces of Versailles, he totally disregards Fränckel's request for advice about public works and employment policies, and instead warns his correspondent against the danger to the Commune from the non-working-class elements determining its course.

All of this did not spare the IWA—and Marx personally—

from being publicly accused of having instigated the uprising of the Commune. The publication of *The Civil War in France* and the public campaign of the IWA after the defeat of the Commune to help the persecuted Communards to escape the brutalities of the provisional government's persecution of the revolt's survivors certainly helped to identify the IWA with the Commune—a position paradoxically embraced both by the European right wing at that time as well as later by the socialist and communist movements.

Identifying the IWA and Marx personally with the Commune was a convenient propaganda tool of the German and French conservative forces, for whom presenting the Commune not as a desperate—and ill-conceived—revolt of Paris radicals but as an international conspiracy concocted by a cabal of revolutionaries in London was politically expedient. Marx's modest public visibility as writer, journalist, and author of *Das Kapital* made his person a convenient target.

It appears that Marx's name became publicly associated with the Commune for the first time in an article published on 19th March 1871 in the extreme right-wing newspaper *Journal de Paris*, which appeared in Versailles. It alleged that Marx had sent a letter to the IWA members in Paris instructing them in detail to start a revolt against the provisional government. The letter attributed to Marx was a blatant forgery, and it appears that the whole idea was inspired by a German adviser then stationed in Versailles, Wilhelm Stieber. Stieber was a Prussian police officer and the chief prosecutor in the Cologne trial against members of the League of Communists in 1852. Stieber was of course familiar with Marx's name, which was mentioned at the trial, and Marx wrote about it from London; so for Stieber this was a sweet revenge for his inability to lock up Marx himself for his—modest—role in 1848–49.

The accusation was picked up by numerous conservative newspapers in Europe. It was then followed by a diplomatic note by Jules Favre, the foreign minister of the provisional government, sent to all of the European powers, claiming that the IWA was responsible for the insurrection of the Commune. This accusation became widely spread, and it moved Marx to write a letter to *The Times* and other papers categorically denying it and referring to the IWA's repeated calls, including in the second address, condemning a revolt against the provisional government. But the denials were, understandably, not always granted credibility, and the relatively wide distribution of *The Civil War in France* did not help these denials, especially in light of the statements in the article that the Commune could, despite its failure and defeat, be viewed as a model for a future socialist society.

The upshot of this extraordinarily complex situation was that, for the first time in his life, Marx became famous as an international revolutionary masterminding a worldwide revolutionary socialist conspiracy.

Marx's attempts to distance the IWA—and himself—from being viewed as responsible for the Commune had of course a practical aim: if governments and public opinion accepted the accusation, the future work of the IWA, which always insisted on working within the confines of the law, might be endangered. Yet on a personal level it appears that Marx drew some satisfaction, albeit a bitter one, from his new fame and notoriety. In a letter to his Hamburg correspondent Ludwig Kugelmann, he wrote ruefully on 18th June 1871:

> I have the honor of being at this moment the best vilified and most menaced man in London. That really does one good after a tedious twenty years' idyll in my den.

Be this as it may, and despite all his encomia about the Commune in *The Civil War in France*, Marx never retreated from his view that the Commune was not a socialist uprising and that, by implication, it had set back the chances of the working-class movement in Europe. Ten years later, in a letter of 22nd February 1881 to the Dutch socialist Ferdinand Domela-Nieuwenhuis, Marx reiterated his view that a socialist government can come into power only if conditions enable it to take all possible measures necessary for transforming society radically, and then, referring to the Commune, added:

> But apart from the fact that it was merely the rising of a city under exceptional conditions, the majority of the Commune was in no way socialist, nor could it be. With a modicum of common sense, however, it could have reached a compromise with Versailles useful to the whole mass of the people— the only thing that could have been reached at the time. The appropriation of the Bank of France alone would have been enough to put an end with terror to the pretensions of the Versailles people, etc. etc.

The political turmoil caused by the Franco-German War and the Paris Commune also had a direct impact on the private life of the Marx family. Marx's daughter Laura and her husband, Paul Lafargue, were caught in the cauldron of the upheaval, and initially managed to stay out of trouble, mainly in Bordeaux. In the summer of 1871, after the defeat of the Commune, Laura's sisters Jenny and Eleanor traveled to Bordeaux and met the couple. The visit did draw the attention of the French authorities, and Jenny and Eleanor were put briefly under temporary arrest, while Lafargue fled to Spain. The two sisters eventually made their way back to London, and Lafargue was able to return to France later, but the incident, though not widely publicized, added a personal worry to Marx's unease about what some members of the French section of the IWA had wrought, through what to him was an irresponsible lack of political judgment.

A NASCENT SOCIAL DEMOCRAT?

Marx had become convinced that the events of the Paris Commune called for serious reassessment as well as organizational reforms if the IWA was to survive. He enjoyed a public standing, both inside and outside the socialist movement, which he had not had before. Part of it, as we have seen, came from the false accusations of him being the leader of the IWA's involvement in the Paris Commune; part came from his growing reputation as the author of *Das Kapital*, which was being translated into Russian and French.

What eventually emerged was not free from personal tensions and animosities, mainly between Marx and Bakunin. This first came to a head in an informal conference of the IWA in London in September 1871, when unsettled conditions in France did not yet allow the convening of a regular congress. A year later, the internal crisis reached its zenith at the IWA Congress held in The Hague in September 1872. This was the Fifth Congress of the association—and was to be its last one. It was also the only congress attended by Marx himself. The issues that were bones of contention between the followers of Marx and of Bakunin can be categorized as organizational, ideological, and ultimately personal.

One of the issues Marx raised at the London meeting called for a change in the IWA rules that explicitly guaranteed the autonomy of each member section of the association. Although the rule was initially meant to allow smooth cooperation among the rather disparate member groups, the experience of the Commune pointed to some dangers involved. Even after the IWA had warned its French members in the second address against an insurrection and called for obedience to the provisional government, members of the French section, mainly the Blaquists, pushed for a revolt, which ended up making the IWA complicit in an act of political violence it had opposed, and branding it as the instigator of the Commune. Against the views of the anarchists and Proudhonists, Marx pushed for a resolution empowering the General Council to decide and direct overall policies, curtailing the autonomy of the individual sections. This move was opposed also by some of the Italian, Spanish, and Swiss sections and led to a nasty fight over accreditation, as Bakunin and his supporters made accusations against what they started calling Marx's authoritarian and dictatorial inclinations. When Marx was elected as corresponding secretary for Russia, this was clearly viewed as a frontal attack on Bakunin.

The other issue was more fundamental and had to do with Marx's insistence that the IWA aimed at organizing the working class for the capture of political power. Bakunin and the Proudhonists objected to these political aims: the revolutionary proletariat, they maintained, should smash all political power, not capture it: Marx was consequently accused of "Statism." When Bakunin intimated that Marx's authoritarian tendencies resulted from his being a Hegelian, a German, and a Jew, the level of argument had indeed slipped considerably.

Those tensions became almost unbridgeable at The Hague Congress. Engels also attended it, and Marx was accompanied by his wife Jenny and daughter Eleanor. His position about the aims of the IWA was clear: for a successful revolution, the proletariat had to take control of the state. This was opposed by Bakunin and his anarchist followers, especially after Marx gave a speech in Amsterdam, accompanying the Congress, that presented a nuanced view of what a proletarian revolution would mean. The speech is a powerful insistence on the need to gain political power but also expresses a highly pluralist approach to the question of how gaining political power would come about—through violent revolution or through peaceful means, shocking the anarchists by maintaining that in some significant cases orderly electoral politics might be the handmaid of socialism.

> The workers must one day conquer political supremacy in order to establish the new organization of labor. . . . But we do not maintain that the attainment of this end requires identical means. We know that one has to take into consideration the institutions, mores [*Sitten*] and traditions of the

different countries, and we do not deny that there are countries like England and America, and if I would be familiar with your institutions, also Holland, where labor may attain its goal by peaceful means.

That this most explicit statement of Marx's mature approach to how socialist transformation could come about appears in the context of a bitter struggle against Bakunin may be of wider significance when one ponders some of the future developments of the revolutionary movement in Russia. Marx viewed with great concern the tendency of Bakunin and his Russian followers to use violence, personal terrorism, and assassination in their activities—a development that came to a head with the assassination of Czar Alexander II in 1881, and much later also accompanied the 1917 revolution. The ugly disagreements at The Hague Congress were also accompanied by the unwillingness of the Bakuninists to accept majority decisions made at the Congress—another feature that would eventually mar the Russian revolutionary movement, culminating in the split between Bolsheviks and Mensheviks.

The debates at The Hague Congress were indeed bitter and vicious. Bakunin and his followers objected to a resolution giving the General Council authority over policy decisions of the individual sections, and challenged the majority that approved it. Consequently, they were expelled from the IWA, so they set up a parallel organization ("The Jura Federation"), which for some time brought together various anarchist associations. At Marx's suggestion, the seat of the General Council was moved to New York, which clearly meant that the IWA no longer believed that it could be the central coordinating focus of a European socialist movement. A few years later it was finally disbanded.

The split and eventual demise of the IWA did not put an end to the debate about the strategy of the working-class movement, and gave rise to venomous public controversies. In 1873,

Bakunin published a Russian volume entitled *Statism and Anarchy*, in which he attacked Marx and his followers, whom he accused of being prisoners of the Prussian state philosophy of the Hegelian school. The critique of Marx is laced with anti-Semitism, and at one point Bakunin argued that Marx on one hand and Disraeli and Rothschild on the other were the heads of the two wings of an international Jewish conspiracy to conquer the world—prefiguring, in a way, what the forged *Protocols of the Elders of Zion* decades later made the cornerstone of their conspiracy theories.

Marx responded to these attacks in a pamphlet a year later, in which he compared Bakunin's anarchist ideology with the ways his movement in Russia actually operated. One of Bakunin's followers, Sergey Nechaev, was put on trial at that time for a number of terrorist acts, and this confirmed Marx's argument that such violent practices would ultimately determine the nature of the revolution once it gained power: a movement based on terror, intimidation, and blackmail will ultimately produce a society based on these methods as well. (Later, Eduard Bernstein, Karl Kautsky, Rosa Luxemburg, and other democratic socialists used these same arguments against the violent Leninist ascent to power.)

Marx's reading of Bakunin's *Statism and Anarchy* reveals what to him was a fundamental contradiction: while Bakunin argues that the anarchists aim at smashing state power and state institutions, his "principles of social order" would in reality introduce a new form of tyranny.

> What a wonderful example of barracks communism! Everything is here—common pots and dormitories, control commissioners and control offices, the regulation of education, production, consumption—in one word, control of all social activity; and at the same time, there appears *Our Committee*, anonymous and unknown, as supreme authority. Surely, this is most pure anti-authoritarianism!

Marx appears here to be pointing out that even apparently radical libertarian ideologies, such as anarchism, can be accompanied by coercive and oppressive tendencies, which he clearly discovers in Bakunin's disdain for any activity that uses the political process with its institutional constraints on power.

The Amsterdam speech is the culmination of a lengthy post-1848 thought process, which led Marx to the conclusion that the proletariat can capture political power through peaceful means. Following economic and social developments in western Europe carefully, he clearly envisages the possibility of an evolutionary path leading the proletariat to the position of the ruling class through extending the suffrage. This reevaluation started quite early after 1849: at the time he was fighting the radical wing among the remnants of the League of Communists in London exile, he considered this possibility in an article printed in the *New York Daily Tribune* on 25th August 1852, entitled "The Chartists."

> The carrying of Universal Suffrage in England would . . . be a far more socialist measure than anything which has been honored with that name on the Continent. Its inevitable result here is *the political supremacy of the working class.*

The reasons for this, he argued, were the existence of a parliamentary system and the disappearance of any traces of a peasantry in England, thus eliminating a basically conservative class from the social fabric of the country.

A decade and a half later, in a much neglected passage of *Das Kapital,* Marx suggested that developments in England were about to be replicated on the Continent, although he suggested that there might be differences and there obviously is no one size that fits all countries.

> In England the process of social upheaval [*Umwältzung*] is palpable. When it has reached a certain point, it must act on the Continent. There it will take a form more brutal or more

humane, according to the degree of development of the working class itself.

This was written in 1867, after the Second Reform Act had opened the way to parliamentary suffrage for a part of the British working class, and suggesting the possibility of a further widening of voting rights. In the same year, on the occasion of the fourth anniversary of the Polish anti-Russian insurrection, Marx reiterated a similar prognosis at a London public meeting:

> It is possible that the struggle between the workers and the capitalists will be less terrible and less bloody than the struggle between the feudal lords and the bourgeoisie in England and France. Let us hope so.

Four years later, Marx was even more emphatic. In an interview published in the American journal *Woodhull & Claflin's Weekly* on 12th August 1871, he said that in Britain the working class needed no violent revolution to achieve political power.

> In England, for example, the way is open for the working class to develop their political power. In a place where they can achieve their goal more quickly and more securely through peaceful propaganda, insurrection would be a folly.

Marx made a similar point in an interview granted to an American journalist and published in the *New York World* on 18th July 1871.

> In England . . . the way to show political power lies open to the working class. Insurrection would be madness where peaceful agitation would more swiftly and surely do the work.

The American reporter who conducted the interview in Marx's house in Hampstead noted that on the table of the pleasant drawing room they were sitting in was displayed "a fine album of Rhine views." They must have included the dramatic and almost mythical Lorelei rock in the Rhine Gorge, the subject of one of Heine's most hauntingly beautiful ballads of that name. That the Rhineland still meant so much to Marx even after having left it more than a quarter century earlier may evoke the equally haunting epigram of the Ukrainian-born Hebrew poet Shaul Tschernichowsky that every person is formed by the design of his homeland's landscape (*ha'adam eyno ela tavnit nof moladeto*). It is fair to guess that when looking at those images in the album, Marx was contemplating not only the stunning physical beauty of his Rhenish homeland, but also what it stood for in history and in the annals of his family. He had no sentimental attachment to Germany; but the Rhineland was a different matter.

Yet it was political developments in Germany that greatly encouraged Marx. The newly established Bismarckian unified Germany extended voting rights for the Reichstag to all male citizens—a tremendous change from the restricted and property-based voting rights in Prussia and other individual German states. Consequently, despite the setbacks caused by the Paris Commune and the virtual demise of the IWA, the new conditions in Germany brought about the emergence of what would eventually become the strongest social democratic party in Europe.

Since the 1860s, there had existed in Germany two working-class parties—the General German Workers Association, founded by Lassalle, and the Social Democratic Workers Party, led by August Bebel and Wilhelm Liebknecht, who were close to Marx. At a congress in the town of Gotha in May 1875, the two parties agreed to merge, forming the German Social Democratic Party (SPD).

A preparatory committee drafted a detailed party program, and one of the drafters sent it to Marx in London for his comments. In his response, Marx maintained that in principle the united party did not need a detailed ideological program: a concise working plan dealing with concrete issues should suffice. But, he added, since a detailed program had been drafted, he

would like to make just a few marginal comments, especially because some publications, mainly at the instigation of Bakunin,
had suggested that Marx and Engels were clandestinely direct-
ing the newly established united party from London, and it
would be important to distance himself from such a claims.

This was the background for what would eventually be
known as Marx's *Critique of the Gotha Program*. His comments
were never made public at the time or even later during his
life, and were virtually disregarded by the founding congress
at Gotha; they had no immediate impact on the united party's
policies. Marx's comments were first published by Engels in
1891, with a preface by him, and thus eventually became part of
the canonical Marx ideological corpus.

Most of Marx's *Critique* is of limited intellectual or historical significance and can be easily dismissed as a typical contribution to the work of a committee drafting a document that
reflects nuances in terminology and approach by two different
socialist traditions—the Marxian and the Lassallean. With some
exasperation and anger—being far away from the action at
Gotha—Marx reiterates his differences with Lassalle's theories
of labor, value, and the role of the state. Many of these comments are petty, trivial, and hair splitting: in a way they cor-
roborate Marx's basic view that the new party should not get
involved too much in ideological arguments.

Despite all this, his comments on the Gotha program include an important section in which he discusses how a future
socialist society would look—a theme he usually avoided as-
siduously, always arguing that this way lies the temptation for
utopian grandstanding. Yet when confronted in the Gotha program with the assertion that once the means of production
would be nationalized, the worker will receive the full value of
his labor, Marx views this as simplistic and wrong-headed. He
then offers perhaps one of his most sophisticated statements of
the complex developmental stages of socialist transformation.

Unsurprisingly, this brings back insights Marx had already expressed in *EPM* of 1844 as well as in *The Communist Manifesto*.

The point Marx is making is not only about stages of development but also about the immanent dialectic of the change. To Marx, for all of its revolutionary nature, the transition from capitalism to socialism will be an outcome of internal changes within capitalist society itself, and not the outcome of a socialist procrustean bed imposed from outside. Hence in its first stage it will still be based on wage labor.

> What we have to deal with here is a communist society not as it has *developed* on its own foundations, but on the contrary, just as it *emerges* from capitalist society, which is thus in every respect, economically, morally, and intellectually, still stamped with the birth marks of the old society from whose womb it emerges. . . . Hence equal right here is still in principle *bourgeois* right. . . . One man is superior to another physically or mentally. . . . This equal right is an unequal right for unequal labor. It recognizes no class differences, because everyone is only a worker like everyone else; but it tacitly recognizes unequal individual endowments. . . . But these defects are inevitable in the first phase of communist society.

So nationalization of the means of production will not by itself provide the abolition of the position of the worker and his relation to his work. This will happen only in the second stage of transformation—and here Marx's language echoes also the soaring rhetoric of his early writings.

> In a higher phase of communist society, after the enslaving subordination of the individual to the division of labor, and therewith also the antithesis between mental and physical labor, have vanished; after labor has become not only a means of life but life's primary need; after the productive forces have also increased with the all-round development of the individual, and all the fountains of co-operative wealth flow more abundantly—only then can the narrow horizon of bour-

geois right be crossed in its entirety and society inscribe on its banners: "From each according to his ability, to each according to his needs."

Just as the text of the Gotha program itself can be easily relegated to oblivion, much of Marx's *Critique of the Gotha Program* could equally accompany it to the same memory hole. But this passage remains one of his most inspiring—and memorable— occasions where he allowed himself a glimpse, vague as it may be, into the realm of the future. With good reason, this remains one of the most quoted passages ever written by Marx—not only as a critic but also as a visionary.

AN INCONGRUOUS ENCOUNTER: MARX AND GRAETZ

Marx's health did not improve over the years, and he continued to suffer from various intestinal maladies as well as boils and constant insomnia. His financial worries were never over, but he could now afford spells at various spas, both in England and later also on the Continent. During 1874–76 he took the waters every summer in Carlsbad in Bohemia, then part of the Austro-Hungarian Empire, accompanied by Eleanor. It so happened that among the people he met there was the German Jewish historian Heinrich Graetz, the founder of modern Jewish historiography and the author of the influential multivolume *History of the Jewish People*. After they met there for the first time, Eleanor contacted Graetz to coordinate their visits to Carlsbad the following year so they would be there at the same time.

We do not have any records of what the two talked about, and there is no surviving substantive correspondence except short notes about prospective dates at Carlsbad. There is an indirect hint that they discussed the political situation in Russia, but one can imagine this was not their only subject of common interest. It would be fascinating to know what these two elderly intellectuals and scholars did talk about—one an ordained Orthodox rabbi who also trained in Leopold von Ranke's school of German historiography, the doyen of modern Jewish historians, and the other by that time the symbol of socialist thought. It is obvious from the very fact that they coordinated their visits to Carlsbad that they found each other's company interesting. Did they question where history in Europe was leading? Did they discuss the possibilities of radical change and revolution? The future of nationalism? German unification? The role of Jews in history? The future of the Jews? Did the ghost of Hegel accompany them to the *Kurhaus* (spa house)? Did Marx confide to Graetz the details of his family's history and the circumstances of his father's conversion? Coming from such diverse backgrounds, and with such totally different biographies, these two sages represented two very different trajectories of Jewish lives in Germany—and in Europe generally—under the complex conditions of emancipation and acculturation; what divided them they also had in common.

We do not know. Yet the Marx-Graetz encounter still awaits the creative talents of a gifted novelist—or playwright—to imagine what the two were talking about when walking side by side from one spring of mineral water to another and sharing their ideas about history, past, present, and possibly future. Such a novel or play could succeed because it would not be concocted out of thin air: hours of insights into philosophy, religion, history did take place: they could be reimagined. Few nineteenth-century intellectual encounters could be more fascinating. Although he was not a Zionist, Graetz's view of the Jews, not as a mere religious community but as a people with a distinct national history, helped prepare the theoretical grid that led to the foundation of Israel, and Marx's thought—for all of its complexity—did pave the way to the Soviet revolution. A more dramatic prefiguration of the encounter between Zion and Kremlin could not be imagined.

Ironically, and yet as could be expected, Austrian imperial police agents did watch Marx during his Carlsbad visits. On 1st September 1875, the local police authorities reported to head-quarters that "Charles Marx, Doctor of Philosophy of London, outstanding leader of the Democratic-Social Democratic Party [*sic*] is again taking the cure" in town. Respectfully the agent reports that, just like during his visit the previous year, "so far Marx has conducted himself quietly and had no great contact with other persons taking the cure and frequently goes for long walks alone." The surveillance obviously missed the walks with Graetz—or the agents did not find they deserved their attention.

9

————◆◆◆————

Toward the Sunset

ON RUSSIA: AGAINST HISTORICAL INEVITABILITY

It may not be surprising that in the last decade of his life, Marx devoted considerable time and effort to Russia. There were two aspects to this: on the one hand, his constant concern about the negative impact Czarist Russia might have on possible progress in the West toward socialism; on the other, the emergence of an active revolutionary movement in Russia itself posed a number of theoretical and practical challenges to Marx's own theories of historical development and revolutionary potentialities. Having basically concluded that western capitalist societies were moving toward transformation through their internal developments that would lead to proletarian hegemony and socialism, turning his attention to Russia was a natural corollary. In his didactic and scholarly method, Marx read voluminously about Russian history and society, and even started learning Russian.

We have seen how since 1849 Marx was worried that an authoritarian and reactionary Russia might again intervene against revolutionary waves in western Europe, as it had done during the Napoleonic Wars and then again in 1848–49. These fears led him to publish a number of articles criticizing, among others, the pro-Russian politics of William Gladstone. In 1877–78, especially after the outbreak of the Russo-Turkish War, he repeated these arguments in a number of articles, both signed and anonymous, taking Gladstone's Liberal Party to task for encouraging the most reactionary regime in Europe and thus overlooking its impact on general European politics. These issues might also have appeared in his conversations with Heinrich Graetz during their visits to Carlsbad. For Graetz the fate of Russia, at that time the home of the largest Jewish population in the world, would obviously be a matter of major concern.

But in the late 1870s and early 1880s political developments in Russia gave rise to a new set of issues. The liberal reforms of Czar Alexander II, whose edict emancipating the serfs in 1861 had totally transformed Russian society, greatly facilitated the emergence of a revolutionary socialist movement in the country. Bakunin's translation of *Das Kapital* into Russian as well as Marx's activity in the IWA, and his international visibility during the Paris Commune, made his name familiar among the Russian revolutionary intelligentsia, many of them students and émigrés in the West. Hence there were numerous references to Marx's writings in the internal debates among Russian radicals about Russia's future developments. In some cases, Russian activists contacted Marx, looking up to him as a master, in typical Russian fashion, which occasionally rubbed him the wrong way, though he was of course flattered by the attention.

One of Marx's most detailed responses to this debate is a lengthy letter—in fact a short essay, in French—that he wrote to the St. Petersburg literary journal *Otechestvennye Zapiski* in November 1877. In it, he referred to a debate among several

Russian intellectuals questioning whether the developments in the West described in *Das Kapital* would have to be repeated in Russia: Would it need to industrialize first and develop a full-blown capitalist society before a future socialist transformation could take place, or could Russia move straight from its pre-capitalist state to a socialist transformation?

Marx took strong exception to the deterministic view that what did happen in the West would have to be replicated in Russia. Acknowledging that Russia had taken some steps in this direction, he was agnostic about whether there was any preor-dained historical necessity that Russia needed to follow the western path. The only conclusion that could be drawn from *Das Kapital*, he argued, was that "if Russia is going to become a capi-talist nation after the example of the West European countries . . . she will not succeed without first transforming a large part of her peasantry into proletarians . . . and once taken into the bosom of the capitalist regime, she will experience its pitiless laws like other profane peoples. That is all."

However, he went on to point out that other paths besides capitalist development were open, bringing up the example of late Roman developments, where the Roman proletariat "be-came not wage earners but a mob of do-nothings, more abject than the 'poor whites' in the American South."

And then Marx referred to an issue that appeared central to Russian revolutionary discourse: Could the historical Russian village commune (the *obshchina*) become the foundation for a new social order in Russia? Among the books on Russia that Marx had read with great interest was a study from the 1830s by the Prussian official August von Haxthausen on the survival of the Russian village communes, and on several occasions he won-dered whether they were still as strong as that work had sug-gested. He mentioned some of the authors who had referred to his own writings and asked whether, when discussing the village communes, they have "found them in Russia, or just in the books of Haxthausen." He further chided these critics, including one in particular, Nikolai Mikhailovsky, for reading too much into *Das Kapital.*

> My critic feels he absolutely must metamorphose my historical sketch of the genesis of capitalism in Western Europe into a historical-philosophical theory of the general path every people is fated to tread, whatever the historical circumstances in which it finds itself. . . . But I beg to differ: he is both honoring and shaming me.

Referring to the different path developments in Rome took, Marx reiterated his insistence on close, comparative historical studies, avoiding recourse to grand historical-philosophical systems.

> Thus events strikingly analogous but taking place in different historical circumstances led to totally different results. By studying each of these forms of evolution separately and then comparing them, one can easily find the clue to this phenomenon, but one will never arrive there by using as one's master-key a general historical-philosophical theory, the supreme virtue of which consists in being super-historical.

This is obviously not only about Russia: it is perhaps Marx's strongest argument about the historicity of his economic analysis, and reflects the same need for pragmatic, comparative studies implied in his differentiated assessment of the modes of socialist transformation expressed in his 1872 Amsterdam speech. Contrary to what later followers claimed, Marx did not have an overall theory of undifferentiated linear universal historical development. In the case of Russia, his argument is clear: *if* Russia develops along capitalist lines, the consequences would be analogous to what had happened in the West. But it was not predetermined that Russia would have to follow the capitalist path—other options were also available and possible.

This pragmatic and open-ended approach, which caused some dismay among Marx's Russian followers—who were looking for ironclad, almost divinely ordained, laws of history—appears again and again in Marx's correspondence with Russian socialists.

The assassination of Alexander II in March 1881 and the resulting brutal repressive countermeasures of the Czarist government threw Russian society—and the various Russian revolutionary groups—into turmoil. These developments also deepened the schism between the Narodnik ("Populist") groups among the revolutionaries, who looked to the peasantry and its communal village traditions, and the so-called "Westernizers," some of whom adopted many of Marx's thoughts. These debates are reflected in repeated questions to Marx by Russian revolutionary activists, and his exchange with Vera Zasulich is perhaps the most interesting. Zasulich was initially a follower of Bakunin, but after spending some time in jail and then reaching the West, she distanced herself from the anarchists and their terrorist tactics. She became one of the founders of the Russian Emancipation of Labor group, and later with George Plekhanov was one of the founders of the Russian Social Democratic Labor Party.

After finding refuge in Switzerland, she addressed Marx on his views about the future of the Russian revolutionary movement, focusing on whether the village communes could become the basis for a future Russian socialist society, thus obviating the western-type path leading through industrialization and the emergence of an industrial proletariat. In other words, could socialism in Russia be based on the peasantry rather than the industrial proletariat, which did not yet exist there in any significant numbers?

Three drafts of Marx's answer have been preserved, as well as the response he eventually sent. His hesitation testifies to his exasperation at being put, by people who viewed themselves as his followers, in the position of having to give doctrinal answers *ex cathedra* to complex and controversial questions. At the same time, it is clear that Marx was himself far from being able to make up his mind: he obviously felt far less comfortable judging Russian conditions, which were then quickly changing, compared with his relative certainties about western European developments.

His letter of 9th March 1881 is far shorter and more peremptory than his initial drafts. It is clear that he would have preferred not to issue a quasi-papal decree. Written in French, the letter's profuse yet distancing courtesy ("*Chère Citoyenne*") masks some of his unease, as does the wordy excuse for the tardiness of his answer. He then quotes three passages from *Das Kapital*, chapter 32, in which he described the development of industrialization in the West, pointing out that all countries in the West followed the same path, yet one should not generalize from this development, as "the 'historical inevitability' of this movement is *expressly Western European.*" If Russia were to follow the West, this would paradoxically mean that common property (that is, the *obshchina*) would have to be transformed into private property—very different from what did happen in the West, where industrialization virtually abolished peasant private holdings.

Yet he still hedges. The question is not a theoretical one, but depends on whether the village commune is in reality strong enough to become the foundation of the new social order.

> The analysis drawn from *Das Kapital* suggests no reasons for or against the vitality of the rural commune; but the social research I conducted . . . has convinced me that this community is the mainspring of Russian social recreation. But in order that it might function as such one would first have to eliminate the deleterious influences which assail it from every quarter and then to ensure the conditions normal for spontaneous development.

This almost delphic pronouncement also reappears in a slightly different form in the ambiguous language Marx and Engels used in January 1882, after the assassination of Alexander II and the ensuing turmoil, in their preface to a new edition of the Russian translation of *The Communist Manifesto*. The first Russian translation of the *Manifesto* was prepared by Bakunin and published in Geneva in the 1860s, in the journal *Kolokol* edited by Alexander Herzen. It had naturally a limited circulation, and after the 1881 events in Russia, Marx and Engels decided, in response to requests from Russian colleagues, and in order to counter Bakunin's anarchist views, to prepare a new edition. In the preface they pointed out, somewhat apologetically, that when the *Manifesto* was drafted in late 1847, Russia was not mentioned, as at that time it "constituted the last great reserve of all European reaction," and in the revolutions of 1848, European princes as well as the bourgeoisie found in Russia "their only salvation." Now, it was claimed, "Russia forms the vanguard of revolutionary action in Europe."

Yet after these encouraging words, obviously meant to bolster the spirit of Russian socialists, Marx's profound doubts and ambivalence about Russia's future prospects return. Indirectly responding to the perennial question posed by Russian revolutionaries whether Russia can proceed toward a socialist revolution based on its traditional peasant village communities without going through western-style industrialization, Marx again gives a hedging answer:

> The only answer possible to that question today is this: If the Russian revolution becomes the signal for a proletarian revolution in the West, so that both complement each other, the present Russian common ownership of land may serve as the starting point for a common development.

Yet in one of his last letters, sent to his daughter Laura, whom he addressed by her family nickname ("Dear Cacadou"),

written on 14th December 1882, he expressed comfort in acknowledging reports from Russia that show "the great run of my
theories in that country," adding that he took great satisfaction
that "I damage a power, which, besides England, is the great
bulwark of the old society."

In retrospect, and one hundred years after the Bolsheviks
seized power in a pre-industrial Russia, with catastrophic and
oppressive results, one can well understand Marx's skeptical
ambivalence.

THE LAST YEARS

An external reason is responsible for the fact that the last
decade of Marx's life is less well documented than previous
years: in September 1870—at the height of the events in France
leading to the Paris Commune—Engels retired from running
his family's business in Manchester and moved to London, to
a spacious house in Regent's Park. In the following years, he
and Marx met almost daily, but this put an end to their voluminous written correspondence, which has been one of the major
sources for the details of Marx's life after he moved to London
in 1849, for he exchanged letters on a constant basis with Engels in Manchester. Once they were both in London, this river
dried up.

Yet it is still possible to reconstruct the last decade of Marx's
life through other sources. Not surprisingly, with his failing
health, this period is characterized by both a diminishing literary output and a somewhat hectic travel schedule between numerous spas and resorts, seeking a cure or at least alleviation
for his numerous maladies. With the demise of the IWA, Marx
was also no longer involved in organizational or institutional
activities.

From more than a century and a half distance, and with the
progress of modern medicine, it is not easy to gain an adequate

diagnosis of Marx's medical history. He had constantly suffered from boils and numerous stomach complaints; over time, heavy coughs, vomiting, and hemorrhages sometimes made speaking and swallowing difficult. Eventually this became accompanied by partial paralysis of one side of his body, some loss of memory, and difficulties in concentration. In all probability, these were the symptoms of latent tuberculosis; his father and some of his siblings had died at an early age from it. The doctors prescribed various treatments and medications, some of which now look totally useless and might even have exacerbated the patient's condition; they also advised various cures and getting away from London's nasty and inclement weather in search of warmer climes and the sun.

So the last years of Marx's life are filled with travels not only to regular spas—we have already mentioned his visits to Carlsbad—but also to numerous other resorts: in some cases he traveled with his wife, in others he was accompanied by his daughter Eleanor; some he undertook on his own.

The list is lengthy: it includes Harrogate, Bad Neuenahr, Ramsgate, Eastbourne, Isle of Wight, Argenteuil (where his daughter Jenny and her husband Charles Longuet lived for some time)—finally even to Algiers, stopping on his way back from there in Cannes and Monte Carlo. Despite Marx's relatively comfortable financial conditions at that time, these travels were obviously expensive, and he needed extra support from Engels, who again helped him generously—for the trip to Bad Neuenahr he supplied him with an extra one hundred pounds. In August 1874, Marx applied for British citizenship, probably to facilitate his travels, but was turned down.

Despite his ailments, Marx tried to keep up both his reading and to a certain degree also his writing. In the late 1870s, Engels was preparing a lengthy polemic against the German social thinker Eugen Dühring, who developed a socialist system criticizing Marx's theories of class analysis and class struggle, mainly arguing that moral persuasion, rather than economic interests, should guide the socialist movement. Marx contributed a chapter to Engels's book, which was initially serialized and then appeared in book form in 1878 and became known as *Anti-Dühring*. It is today mainly remembered for Engels's shrewd remark—aimed mainly at Bakunin's anarchists—that under socialism the state would not be abolished but would "wither away." That Dühring's works later laid the foundations for a populist racist anti-Semitism made the polemic even more central in the canon of Marxist socialism. Marx's contribution to Engels's study became his last major piece of writing; his later years left only letters and sporadic manuscript notes.

During these years, because of Marx's failing health, European—and mainly German—socialists traveled to London to meet him: Wilhelm Liebknecht, Karl Kautsky, and others went on what started to become known as the pilgrimage to London.

On 2nd December 1881, Marx's wife, Jenny, died of cancer. Marx himself was too ailing to attend her funeral. Jenny's death took a further toll on his health, and in desperation his doctors urged him to follow the sun—to Algiers, of all places, which had become fashionable among French people suffering from lung ailments. This was Marx's only trip outside of western Europe, and his impressions from his visit in the winter months of 1882—as far as one can glean from a number of rather disjointed letters to his family and friends—were mixed.

On one hand, Marx enthused about the lush Mediterranean winter landscape, and the "Babel of Moors, Arabs, Berbers, Turks and Negroes," which, he wrote, would have been a joy to his beloved grandson. But he was not unaware of the political and historical context, which he referred to with his customary perspicacity. He showed some understanding for the Muslim Arabs' hatred toward their French rulers and "their hope for an ultimate victory over these infidels." On the other hand, he noticed the fact that the black Africans of the region had been enslaved by the Arabs, and that it was French colonial rule that put an end to this racial slavery and emancipated the blacks. As in his writings about India, there is no bleary-eyed naive idealization of the Noble Savage.

Yet the medical results of this rather extraordinary journey to Algiers were meager. With his daughter Laura, he took further trips to Switzerland, and in the winter he went to the Isle of Wight.

And then tragedy struck again: on 11th January 1883, his eldest daughter, Jenny, who was married to the French socialist Charles Longuet, died in Paris, also from cancer, at age forty.

Marx never recovered from this shock. Two months later, on 14th March 1883, he died at his home in Hampstead.

The funeral took place on 17th March at Highgate Cemetery in North London, where he was buried next to his wife Jenny. A lengthy report on the funeral, written and signed by Engels, appeared on 22nd March in the German *Der Sozialdemokrat.*

Speaking in English, Engels opened his eulogy dramatically: "On the 14th of March, at a quarter to three in the afternoon, the greatest living thinker ceased to think." It was as a revolutionary thinker, not as an activist, that Engels primarily eulogized his colleague and lifelong friend, going on to anchor Marx's life achievement in the way he was to memorialize him in the following years: as the founder of scientific socialism (a term hardly ever used by Marx himself). Marx's death, Engels declared, was an "immeasurable loss both to the militant proletariat of Europe and America and to historical science," making the questionable parallel with Darwin, as we have already seen. He recalled Marx's various editorial positions and his journalistic writings. *The Communist Manifesto* was not mentioned, but he praised Marx as the founder of the IWA—obviously bending the record considerably. *Das Kapital* was not mentioned explicitly, but Marx's scholarly studies of the contradictions of capitalism and the eventual victory of the proletariat were.

In an understandable exaggeration, Engels called Marx "the best-hated and most calumniated man of his time," commenting rather generously that "though he may have had many opponents he had hardly one personal enemy."

It was a bravado speech, well attuned to the political goals and needs of the socialist movement at the time. It was later translated into many languages, appearing in most editions of Marx and Engels's *Selected Works* and becoming for generations the official narrative of Marx's life and achievements. Engels knew what he was doing: laying the foundations for what became the pyramidal structure of Marx's hagiography and establishing him as the major thinker of the socialist movement. As funeral orations go, it is indeed splendid, and deserves to be remembered next to Pericles' Oration in the Peloponnesian War and Lincoln's Gettysburg Address.

As Engels reported, two wreaths were laid at the grave—by the editorial board of *Der Sozialdemokrat* and by the London Workers Educational Society. Marx's son-in-law Charles Longuet then read three telegrams—from Piotr Lavrov in Paris on behalf of Russian socialists, the French Workers Party, and the Madrid branch of the Spanish Workers Party.

Finally, Wilhelm Liebknecht, who traveled from Cologne, delivered a eulogy in the name of the German Social Democratic Party. In his report, Engels also mentioned that "the natural sciences were represented by two celebrities," naming two mildly known scientists—a zoologist and a chemist—who had been close to Marx personally but could hardly be described as representing the scientific community.

What Engels did not report was that there were just eleven people at the funeral.

10

A Historical Perspective: Impact and Legacy

WHEN THE German Social Democratic historian Franz Mehring was preparing his biography of Karl Marx in the early years of the twentieth century, he visited London to try to interview people who had known Marx during his lifetime. It is told that he found in an old-age home a former librarian of the British Museum Reading Room, who vaguely remembered Marx when shown his photograph, and then added: "Oh yes, Dr Marx, a very fine gentleman indeed. For years he used to come to the Reading Room almost every day, but then one day he stopped coming and nobody has ever heard of him again."

This is of course both funny but also ridiculous, and for all the understandable hyperbole of Engels's encomium in his funeral oration, that "Marx's name will endure through the ages, and so will his work," this seems to be much closer to the truth. Yet Marx's impact is more complex and paradoxical than that of any major modern thinker, and has to be traced not only in the realm of political development, but also in terms of its influence on various fields of human thinking, research, and public discourse.

First and foremost, capitalism did not collapse—on his major prognosis, Marx was wrong. Yet the current global free market system is very different from the sort of capitalism he described in *The Communist Manifesto* or *Das Kapital*. In order to survive their intrinsic tensions and cyclical crises, so acutely described by Marx, capitalist societies introduced significant reforms and adjustments. Capitalist economies as he described them were premised on the principle of total nonintervention by the state in the economy: yet toward the end of the nineteenth century, and even more after the financial crisis of the 1920s and 1930s and World War II, social welfare reforms gave workers significant protection from the brutalities of early capitalism; legislation limited working hours and the employment of children and women; and unemployment, medical, and old age insurance offered meaningful protections, as did paid vacations and other welfare measures. No longer could it be said that proletarians had nothing to lose but their chains.

That some of these protective reforms were initially introduced by conservative statesmen like Bismarck and Disraeli just adds to the dialectical twists of historical development: Marx himself did acknowledge in *Das Kapital* that, especially in England, extensive factory legislation might pave the way for a peaceful transformation. The growing power of the trade unions—no longer legally prohibited as interfering with the unrestricted play of market forces—coupled with the widening of the suffrage helped empower socialist parties. The modern welfare state was further extended through the writings of John Maynard Keynes and the New Deal under Franklin D. Roosevelt. Wistfully it can be argued that Marx's dire prophesies about the doom of unbridled free market capitalism have been taken seriously and absorbed by the powers-that-be, thus making it possible for the capitalist system to reform defensively and survive, albeit it in a much milder form. Contrary developments under Ronald Reagan and Margaret Thatcher weakened some of these achievements, but they did not do away with its major premises. A totally unregulated free market does not exist anymore anywhere.

This had a further consequence: in the first half of the twentieth century, Marx's thought inspired some of the best intellectual minds in the western world, but such a fascination with radical social revolution is no longer a central factor in the political life of western societies. There may be other challenges to these societies, but these are very different from the doomsday scenarios of the *Manifesto*. Similarly, because of globalization, so aptly described there by Marx, much of industrial production migrated to Third World countries, with their lower wages and almost nonexistent factory and welfare legislation. Consequently, an exploited and pauperized industrial proletariat has almost totally disappeared from western societies, taking with it the revolutionary potential it once embodied; most of the classical working class in the West is now safely ensconced in the middle class.

On the other hand, Marx's name became associated with the major revolutionary attempt to establish a communist society— the Soviet Union. We have seen how ambivalent Marx was about Russia and its revolutionary prospects. Yet one thing is clear: Lenin's October Revolution happened under conditions totally different from those ever envisaged by Marx.

For one, it took place in the context of a country in the throes of a war that led to defeat and delegitimization of its czarist system: it was not a popular revolt against the ruling classes and was led by a small group of revolutionaries, not a mass working-class movement. Moreover, it took place in a society that was still pre-modern and pre-industrialized, with a weak proletariat and a vast peasantry that was far from being radicalized. The oppressive path taken by the Russian Revolution was a direct outcome of these conditions, exacerbated by the fact that, on taking power, the Bolsheviks did exactly the opposite of what Marx had envisaged a socialist revolutionary government should do: instead of the Ten Regulations of the *Manifesto*, which called for the nationalization of private property in land but the slow and step-by-step transfer of industrial property to the state, the Soviets confiscated the estates of the aristocracy and distributed them to the vast peasant population in order to gain their support, while at the same time nationalizing all industrial property. The consequences were catastrophic, leading eventually to the forced collectivization of peasant property and the forced industrialization of the Five-Year Plans. The chaos, disruption, and need for extreme coercive measures doomed the Soviet Revolution to the horrors of Stalinism; its emancipatory dream turned into the nightmare of the gulag.

In order to survive, Lenin's government not only got out of the war, but also signed a separate peace treaty with Germany and its allies during the winter of 1918. The Treaty of Brest-Litovsk gave imperial Germany its war aims in the east: Poland, Ukraine, and the Baltics, in one way or another, came under German hegemony. This *Drang nach Osten* (drive to the east) was what German militarism was fighting for under Generals Paul von Hindenburg and Erich Ludendorff, and it was achieved through a peace treaty with a Russian revolutionary government.

This put the German Social Democratic Party in an impossible position. At the outbreak of the war in 1914, and after much soul searching, the reformist German SPD—the largest party in the German Reichstag—voted for the war credits with a clear caveat that it opposed any territorial expansion or annexation. It was not an easy position to take, and it led to a schism in the party, resulting in the secession of its pacifist left wing.

With the Treaty of Brest-Litovsk, a radical revolutionary government, claiming Marx as its prophet, acceded to imperial

Germany's most extreme expansionist policies. The German right wing had always viewed the SPD as anti-national and un-patriotic; now it became almost a laughingstock, as radical socialists in Russia paved the way for German imperialism in the east, while German social democrats were against annexations. Part of the problem faced by the SPD-led governments after 1918 can be traced to the delegitimation accusations they faced in the wake of Brest-Litovsk.

There is another aspect to all of this: during the Cold War, many anti-communists ascribed the oppressive measures of the Soviet system to Marx's ideology. As we have seen, there is very little support for such an interpretation in Marx's own writings. In retrospect, however, it is now clear that many of the repressive Soviet measures not only resulted from the attempt to force a socialist mold on a pre-industrial society, but also had deep roots in the authoritarian traditions of Russian statecraft and the country's weak civil society—an issue Marx himself addressed in his polemic against Bakunin. This dynamic continues to haunt Russia today: the quick reversal from the liberalizing goals of Mikhail Gorbachev's *perestroika* to the authoritarian methods of Vladimir Putin suggests that the continuity—and deep-rooted presence—of traditional czarist structures and methods is the major determinant of Russian political development, under Lenin and Stalin as well as Putin. A similar analysis can be made for the Confucian authoritarian traditions that are currently the backbone of the remaining communist regimes in China, Vietnam, and North Korea. They may invoke Marx's name, but their roots, internal legitimacy—and sustainability—are somewhere else.

The eventual collapse of the Soviet Union was a direct corollary of the circumstances of Lenin's accession to power and the unavoidable failure of the attempt to realize in a pre-industrialized society Marx's analysis and project, which as he himself had repeatedly emphasized, were grounded in the conditions of western European societies. The coercive imposition of Soviet-style communism on Eastern European countries after 1945 gave rise to regimes with a total lack of legitimacy and local support: the repeated anti-communist uprisings, in East Germany, Poland, Hungary, and Czechoslovakia, only prefigured the quick implosion of these regimes when they were deprived after 1989 of the support of the Soviet bayonets that had put them in power in the first place after World War II.

But even though in the purely political realm, Marx's thought cannot claim many achievements beyond the defensive measures aimed at preventing his own prophecies of doom, his impact on other major fields of human activity are enormous, and cannot be denied.

Marx's writings have dramatically revolutionized historical, social, cultural, and economic research. Since Marx, one cannot write history without acknowledging and researching the links between economic issues and political structures. As Marx himself showed in his meticulous analysis of post-1848 French and German political developments, one does not have to follow the dichotomic polarization theories of the *Manifesto* to realize how economics and politics are structurally interwoven. Sociology and anthropology owe debts to Marx that are not always acknowledged. "Alienation" figures centrally in sociology and psychology, while in philosophy and religious studies the way Marx developed his theories of alienation plays a central role: Catholic liberation theology is unthinkable without his input. And political economy, following in the steps of Marx without always being doctrinally encumbered by him, is now part and parcel of the way economics is academically presented. These disciplines, as well as law and various aspects of literary studies, can now be said to stand on the shoulders of Marxian analysis, even if many of their protagonists may quarrel with his conclusions. What Plato has been to classical philosophy, Marx is to modern studies in the humanities. Some of this may occasionally appear as uncritical infatuation, but it cannot be denied how much Marx has impacted modern scholarship.

There are two paradoxes involved in this: the growing presence of Marx in academic and intellectual discourse has been accompanied by the decline of Marxian-oriented political activity, mainly the weakening of trade unions and working-class political parties in modern industrialized societies. It sometimes appears as if the academic salience of Marx's legacy may be a substitute for the political diminution of his action-oriented philosophy, a return, so to speak, to "idealist" Hegelian positions: some who despaired of political radical activism may have found refuge in the halls of academe. Yet despite the fact that it is obvious that critical theory in university English departments is a poor alternative to mounting the barricades, Marx's presence in the intellectual discourses of so many fields of human activity is a powerful testimony to the force of his theories, and it does have an influence, albeit an indirect one, on political and social development.

This is accompanied by the fact that Marx's impact on contemporary intellectual discourse does not draw in most cases on what have been considered his canonical writings as published, republished, commented upon, and translated into tens of languages as part of his standard *Selected Works*. Most of his influence comes from the publication of his manuscripts that Engels did not see fit to include in the canon: mainly the *Economic-Philosophical Manuscripts* of 1844, as well as the various unpublished drafts of *Das Kapital*, eventually published as the *Grundrisse*, as well as *The German Ideology*, published by Engels somewhat reluctantly and with obvious reservations.

This was the second posthumous flourishing of Marx's writings, after the first one initiated by the editorial efforts of Engels in the 1890s. To a large extent this saved Marx—and his legacy—from the decline of political Marxist-oriented parties and movements. It helped Marx's thought to transcend the immediate—and ephemeral—circumstances of its historical origins and made it into a classic of human thinking of lasting value.

In the language of his eleventh thesis on Feuerbach, Marx evidently helped to interpret the world in different ways—as well as to change it. Yet both his interpretation and the changes it wrought turned out to be somewhat different from what he had envisaged himself. But true to his dialectical thinking, he would not have been surprised.

Epilogue: Distant Echoes?

AMONG THE MANY ARTICLES Marx wrote for the *New York Daily Tribune* on European politics was one about the outbreak of the Crimean War. It was published on 15th April 1854, and in it Marx gave a detailed account of the inner composition of society in the Ottoman Empire—issues not well known in Europe, let alone across the Atlantic. He further explained the *millet* system under which non-Muslim communities, Christian and Jewish, were allowed a degree of internal autonomy and self-government in matters of personal status and control of their places of worship and religious shrines. Marx's account is informative and appears well researched.

Since one of the *casus belli* leading to the Crimean War had to do with conflicting claims to custody over certain areas in the Church of the Holy Sepulcher in Jerusalem, toward the end of his article Marx offered a concise profile of the city. The passage starts with the following demographic data:

The sedentary population of Jerusalem numbers about 15,500 souls, of which 4,000 are Mussulmans [Muslims] and 8,000 Jews. The Mussulmans, forming about a fourth part of the whole, and consisting of Turks, Arabs, and Moors, are, of course, the masters in every respect.

After this statement which points out that even under Turkish Muslim rule the Jews constituted a majority in Jerusalem, Marx continues in his correct, though not always idiomatic English, to make the following somewhat surprising description of the Jewish community in Jerusalem, not actually relevant to the main theme of an article dealing with causes of the Crimean War:

> Nothing equals the misery and the suffering of the Jews at Jerusalem, inhabiting the most filthy quarter of the town, called *haret-el-yahoud*, in the quarter of dirt, between Zion and the Moriah, where their synagogues are situated—the constant objects of Mussulman oppression and intolerance, insulted by the Greeks, persecuted by the Latins [that is, Catholics], and living only upon the scant alms transmitted by their European brethren. The Jews, however, are not natives, but from different and distant countries, and are only attracted to Jerusalem by the desire of inhabiting the Valley of Jehoshaphat, and to die on the very place where the redemption is to be expected. "Attending their death," says a French author, "they suffer and pray. Their regards turned to that mountain of Moriah, where once rose the Temple of Lebanon, and which they dare not approach, they shed tears on the misfortunes of Zion and their dispersion over the world."

This is surely an extraordinary passage in its empathy for the small and beleaguered Jewish community in Jerusalem. No similar sentiments about any other Jewish community anywhere else can be found in Marx's voluminous oeuvre.

In 1976, as director-general of Israel's Ministry of Foreign Affairs, I headed the Israeli delegation to the UNESCO General Assembly meeting that year in Nairobi. At that time Israel was under attack at UNESCO by the Arab countries and their Soviet and Islamic allies, which had been making accusations that its archeological excavations in East Jerusalem, captured from Jordan in the Six-Day War of 1967, were neglecting the non-Jewish layers of the city's history—Roman, Byzantine, Omayyad, Crusader, and Ottoman—in an attempt, it was asserted, to "Judaize" Jerusalem. Israel was on the verge of being expelled from UNESCO, and one of the major items of the Nairobi assembly was devoted to Jerusalem.

The legal counsel's office of the ministry provided a legal—or should I say highly legalistic—brief for my speech at the assembly. I decided to add it to the assembly's documentation but to pursue a different approach in my speech to the plenary session.

My argument was that obviously Jerusalem has a complex and multi-religious history, but the claim that Israel was trying to "Judaize" Jerusalem was absurd. The fact of the matter is that in modern times there has been—even before the advent of Zionism—a Jewish majority in the city, as testified by many nineteenth-century travelers and writers. I then moved to quote from Marx's article, which clearly states that Jerusalem had a Jewish majority as far back as the mid-nineteenth century. But I introduced the Marx passage without naming him, merely referring to it as a description written "by one of the most important nineteenth-century thinkers, viewed by some as THE most important thinker of that century." Then, after I finished reading the lengthy passage, I added: "As I hope our Soviet colleagues realize, I was quoting from an 1854 article by Karl Marx."

And then the incredible happened: a member of the Soviet delegation sprang up, interrupting me, and shouted: "This is a forgery! Marx never wrote this!" Still at the speaker's podium, I took out the volume I was reading from, showed it to the audience, and said: "I am quoting from this volume published in

Moscow by the Soviet official Foreign Languages Publishing House. I am sure the Soviet delegate is not implying that an official Soviet publication is involved in a forgery of a text by Karl Marx."

I can still relish the general outburst of loud laughter in the hall. Eventually, with the help of western delegations, we managed to work out a formula that enabled Israel to continue its excavations with an accompanying UNESCO presence.

The same evening, at a reception at the Canadian embassy, two persons in Mao jackets approached me. The younger, obviously the interpreter, introduced the older person as the head of the delegation of the People's Republic of China (at that time Israel did not have diplomatic relations with Beijing). With a wry smile, the senior Chinese delegate said: "We may not agree with the political points you made at the General Assembly. But we always like when someone quotes Karl Marx to the Soviets." I thanked him, commenting that it sometimes does help to be acquainted with what Marx actually said and wrote.

There is a coda to this, and it relates to a further passage from the same article, which I did not quote in Nairobi:

> To make these Jews more miserable, England and Prussia appointed, in 1840, an Anglican bishop at Jerusalem, whose avowed object is their conversion. He was dreadfully thrashed in 1845, and sneered at alike by Jews, Christians and Turks. He may, in fact, be stated to have been the first and only cause of union between all the religions at Jerusalem.

This cryptic statement needs some elaboration. The reference is to the first Anglican bishop of Jerusalem, indeed appointed jointly by the Church of England and the Prussian Lutheran *Landeskirche* with the explicit mandate from the London Society for the Conversion of the Jews to try to convert members of the Jewish community of Jerusalem. The bishop appointed by the two Protestant churches was the Reverend

Michael Solomon Alexander, himself a converted Jew from Posen (Poznán), then in Prussia. He was born Michael Wolff, immigrated to England, where he served first as a rabbi in Norwich and later converted and was ordained as a priest in the Church of England. His thrashing—almost certainly by members of the Jewish community—became a minor cause célèbre in mid-nineteenth-century Jerusalem.

Perhaps one should not read too much into these passages: neither into Marx's statement that the Jews make up the largest religious community in Jerusalem, nor into his extraordinary description of their suffering and messianic longings connected to the Holy City and the Temple Mount. Maybe one should not even attach too much significance to his evident *Schadenfreude* at the humiliations of a Jew converted to Christianity who saw his life mission in drawing his former co-religionists, and in Jerusalem of all places, away from their ancestral attachment and lead them into the salvationist bosom of Christianity. But being aware of the convoluted history of Marx's family conversion, one may still wonder.

Despite Marx's political and intellectual prominence, there still is no complete and full critical edition of his works, nor does there exist one authoritative English translation of all his writings. Numerous partial editions of his works have been published over the years, initially by editors connected to the German Social Democratic Party and then under the auspices of various Soviet institutions. Under these circumstances their selection and editing reflected in many cases their respective political orientations and agendas.

Most of Marx's work was written in German, but he also wrote some of his pieces in English, mainly the dozens of articles he submitted for publication in the *New York Daily Tribune;* so also were the addresses he prepared in the 1860s and 1870s on behalf of the International Workingmen's Association, most notably his account of the Paris Commune (*The Civil War in France*). An English version of *The Communist Manifesto* was prepared and published under Marx's own supervision; and shortly after his death an English translation of volume 1 of *Das Kapital* was overseen by Engels.

The most well known and widely distributed English collection of Marx and Engels's *Selected Works* was published in two volumes in the 1960s in Moscow by the Institute of Marxism-Leninism of the Central Committee of the Communist Party of the Soviet Union, accompanied by an edition of *Selected Correspondence*. It was highly selective, did not include any of Marx's early writings, and lacked a scholarly apparatus. In many cases it was also a faulty and tendentious translation.

Over the years other, more reliable partial translations have appeared. Among them the following should be mentioned: Karl Marx and Friedrich Engels, *Basic Writings on Philosophy and Politics*, edited by Lewis S. Feuer (Garden City, N.Y., 1959); Karl Marx, *Early Writings*, edited by T. B. Bottomore (London, 1963); *The Portable Marx*, edited by Eugene Kamenka (New York, 1983); Karl Marx, *Early Political Writings*, edited by Joseph O'Malley (Cambridge, England, 1994); Karl Marx, *Later Political Writings*, edited by Terrell Carver (Cambridge, England, 1996).

The first attempt to publish a full critical edition of the works of Marx and Engels was initiated in the 1920s in the Soviet Union, entitled *Marx-Engels-Gesamtausgabe* [Marx-Engels Complete Edition] (*MEGA*), under the editorial direction of David Riazanov and later Vladimir Adoratsky. It was discontinued during the Stalinist purges, with tragic consequences for some of the editors (Riazanov was arrested, put on trial, and executed).

In the 1960s the Institute for Marxism-Leninism in East Berlin, German Democratic Republic, published a forty-volume edition of Marx and Engels's works (*Marx-Engels Werke*). It followed a Soviet, Russian-language edition and at the time of its publication was the most extensive collection available of the works of Marx and Engels. It still lacked an adequate critical apparatus; articles, books, and letters written by Marx in English or French appeared not in the original language but in a German translation, and no attempt was made to compare published versions with original manuscripts available in various archives. It was this incomplete edition that became the basis for the English-language *Collected Works* of Marx and Engels, published beginning in 1976. This edition contains many of the faults of the East German *Werke* (and its Russian editorial origins), as well as in many cases questionable translations, is still highly selective, and of course despite its title is far from being a complete edition of Marx's works.

One of the major faults of these Soviet-inspired editions is that in presenting the works of Marx and Engels as one canonical corpus they do intellectual injustice to their separate identity as distinct persons and authors.

It is because of the lack of one authoritative English translation, and the history of previous problematic and sometimes conflicting translations, that for this volume I have rendered my own translations of quotations from Marx's German texts, consulting existing translations for possible guidance. In addition, this avoids the tendentious translations which in many cases have helped to distort the way Marx's thinking has been perceived over the years. Two examples will suffice: Marx makes central use in his theoretical writings of the Hegelian term *bürgerliche Gesellschaft*, and it is a serious question whether and when this should be translated as "bourgeois society" or "civil society" (although certainly not as "bourgeoisie"). Similarly, the term *Judentum*, as it appears in his pivotal essay "Zur Judenfrage," should obviously be translated as "Judaism," and not as "Jewry" or "Jewishness."

Passages from works that Marx wrote and published in English are, of course, quoted in his original version, as are works that were translated under his supervision (including *The Communist Manifesto* and *The Civil War in France*). Occasionally this results in somewhat archaic or stilted language that he used.

The effort to provide a full critical edition of all of Marx's writings is currently under way in an ongoing project—*Marx-Engels-Gesamtausgabe-2* (also known as *MEGA-2*). This edition is being prepared by the Internationale Marx-Engels Stiftung (IMES), a joint enterprise of the International Institute of Social History in Amsterdam and the Academy of Sciences of Berlin-Brandenburg. Until now more than fifty volumes have appeared, containing not only the necessary apparatus but also comparisons of text variants from different editions, comparisons of various drafts, and a detailed publication history of each item; a similar number of volumes is still to appear. The editorial policy followed by *MEGA-2* has also been to try to decouple the long-established tradition of treating Marx and Engels as virtually one single author. This is aimed at restoring to each of them his own discrete identity and integrity, despite their decades'-long close cooperation.

I have served for years as a member of the international Scientific Advisory Board of this enterprise and can not only attest to its enormous scope, bringing together dozens of scholars from all over the world, but have also witnessed the incredible challenges of liberating Marx from more than a century of partisan tendencies and political entanglements. In preparing my English translations of quotations from Marx's work for this volume, I have used, whenever available, the original texts as published in *MEGA-2*.

For Further Reading

Isaiah Berlin, *Karl Marx* (new edition, Princeton, 2013); William Clare Roberts, *Marx's Inferno: The Political Theory of Capital* (Princeton, 2016); Sidney Hook, *From Hegel to Marx* (Ann Arbor, 1962); Eugene Kamenka, *The Ethical Foundations of Marxism* (London, 1961); George Lichtheim, *Marxism* (London, 1961); Herbert Marcuse, *Reason and Revolution* (New York, 1954); David McLellan, *Karl Marx: His Life and Thought* (new edition, London, 2006); Jonathan Sperber, *Karl Marx: A Nineteenth-Century Life* (New York/London, 2013); Gareth Stedman Jones, *Karl Marx: Greatness and Illusion* (Cambridge, Massachusetts, 2016); Robert Tucker, *Philosophy and Myth in Karl Marx* (Cambridge, 1961); Francis Wheen, *Karl Marx* (London, 2010).

ACKNOWLEDGMENTS

I would like to thank Anita Shapira and Steven Zipperstein, editors of the Jewish Lives series, for suggesting that I consider writing the volume on Karl Marx. When Anita Shapira first approached me with the idea, I had my doubts whether I would like to revisit Marx's life and thought many years after I had first addressed them. But after a sleepless night I decided that I should deal with issues and aspects of Marx's Jewish background that I had consciously avoided at the time. I am grateful to both of them and to Ileene Smith, the editorial director of the series, for all their support and encouragement.

My further thanks go to Heather Gold and Phillip King of Yale University Press, who have accompanied me during various stages of writing and editing. Their patience with me and their understanding for the need to deal with some tricky issues growing out of the extraordinary role Marx played during the past two centuries of world history made my work easier and the book's completion possible. I wish all authors should have such editors accompanying their work.

INDEX

Jewish Lives is a prizewinning series of interpretative biography designed to explore the many facets of Jewish identity. Individual volumes illuminate the imprint of Jewish figures upon literature, religion, philosophy, politics, cultural and economic life, and the arts and sciences. Subjects are paired with authors to elicit lively, deeply informed books that explore the range and depth of the Jewish experience from antiquity to the present.

Jewish Lives is a partnership of Yale University Press and the Leon D. Black Foundation. Ileene Smith is editorial director. Anita Shapira and Steven J. Zipperstein are series editors.

Primo Levi: The Matter of a Life, by Berel Lang
Groucho Marx: The Comedy of Existence, by Lee Siegel
Menasseh ben Israel: Rabbi of Amsterdam, by Steven Nadler
Moses Mendelssohn: Sage of Modernity, by Shmuel Feiner
Harvey Milk: His Lives and Death, by Lillian Faderman
Moses: A Human Life, by Avivah Zornberg
Proust: The Search, by Benjamin Taylor
Yitzhak Rabin: Soldier, Leader, Statesman, by Itamar Rabinovich
Walter Rathenau: Weimar's Fallen Statesman, by Shulamit Volkov
Jerome Robbins: A Life in Dance, by Wendy Lesser
Julius Rosenwald: Repairing the World, by Hasia R. Diner
Mark Rothko: Toward the Light in the Chapel,
    by Annie Cohen-Solal
Gershom Scholem: Master of the Kabbalah, by David Biale
Solomon: The Lure of Wisdom, by Steven Weitzman
Steven Spielberg: A Life in Films, by Molly Haskell
Alfred Stieglitz: Taking Pictures, Making Painters, by Phyllis Rose
Barbra Streisand: Redefining Beauty, Femininity, and Power,
    by Neal Gabler
Leon Trotsky: A Revolutionary's Life, by Joshua Rubenstein
Warner Bros: The Making of an American Movie Studio,
    by David Thomson

FORTHCOMING TITLES INCLUDE:

Hannah Arendt, by Peter Gordon
Judah Benjamin, by James Traub
Irving Berlin, by James Kaplan
Franz Boas, by Noga Arikha
Mel Brooks, by Jeremy Dauber
Bob Dylan, by Ron Rosenbaum
Elijah, by Daniel Matt